UNDOING THE BUSH-CHENEY LEGACY
A TOOL KIT FOR CONGRESS & ACTIVISTS

MCLI Little Orange Book Series:

1. "Landmark Cases Left Out of Your Textbooks" (2006)
2. "The Living Constitution" (2007)
3. "Undoing the Bush-Cheney Legacy: A Tool Kit for Congress and Activists" (Dec. 26, 2008)
4. "The Universal Declaration of Human Rights Is The Law: A Guide to U.D.H.R. Articles in Treaties Ratified by the U.S." (Dec. 10, 2008)

Other books by MCLI:

"Continuing Legal Education: Using Office of Inspector General and 3 Ratified Treaties" (2008)

"Challenging U.S. Human Rights Violations after 9/11" (2005)

"How To Use 'New' Civil Rights Laws after 9/11" (2003)

"Nuclear Weapons Are Illegal: The Historic Opinion of the World Court and How It Will Be Enforced" (1998)

"Alexander Meiklejohn: Teacher of Freedom" (1981)

UNDOING THE BUSH-CHENEY LEGACY

A TOOL KIT
FOR CONGRESS & ACTIVISTS

EDITED BY ANN FAGAN GINGER

Published 2008 by Meiklejohn Civil Liberties Institute

Inquiries should be addressed to

Meiklejohn Civil Liberties Institute

P.O. Box 673

Berkeley, CA 94701-0673

Phone : (510) 848-0599

Fax: (510) 848-6008

www.mcli.org

Library of Congress Cataloging-in-Publication Data
ISBN Number 978-0-913876-24-4

Second Edition, December 2008

UNDOING THE BUSH-CHENEY LEGACY
A Tool Kit For Congress and Activists

Contents

INTRODUCTION TO THE TOOL KIT

The new Congress has the power -- and the duty -- to repeal or amend all laws adopted and all "laws" stated or enforced during the Bush-Cheney Administration that violate basic U.S. law.

These "laws" run from A to W -- from Agriculture to Wars in Afghanistan and Iraq, and ... There are so many of these "laws" that each one must be described briefly so this booklet will be handy to use -- in making presentations to Congress, the public, and the media.

Many of these laws are statutes proposed by Bush-Cheney, passed by the House and Senate, signed by Bush, funded in the next Bush budget passed by Congress.[1] Other "laws" are signing statements.

These Bush "laws" ignore basic laws found in the U.S. Constitution, particularly the "promote the general welfare" clause, the Ninth Amendment protection of "other[...] rights retained by the people," the Bill of Rights, and the Reconstruction Amendments 13 and 14. "Bush laws" also violate international human rights standards and peace law in treaties that are part of the "supreme law of the land" under the U.S. Constitution (Art. VI, cl. 2). These treaties were signed by the President and ratified by the U.S. Senate: the United Nations Charter (1945), the International Covenant on Civil and Political Rights (ICCPR) (1992); the International Convention Against Torture and other Cruel, Inhuman or Degrading Treatment or Punishment (ICAT) (1994); and the International Convention on Elimination of all forms of Racial Discrimination (ICERD) (1994).

To start enforcing the law again, not "the law" stated by Bush-Cheney, the House and Senate can immediately quit funding for projects established by Bush Executive Orders and funding for Blackwater. See April 2007 book by John C. Conyers & Elizabeth Holtzman, "The Constitution In Crisis."[2]

Some of Bush "laws" are Executive Orders or Signing Statements by the President that the new President can immediately invalidate. The House and Senate can also pass Sen. Specter's Presidential

1

Signing Statement Act[3] that instructs federal courts to ignore signing statements and decide based on the Rules of Construction in the Acts as passed by Congress.

The House and Senate can also pass budgets that specifically do not fund certain department and commission actions initiated under Bush-Cheney that are against the law, including projects of NAFTA and NATO.[4] And they can resolve that the new President should not renew any of the Status of Forces Agreements that Bush and previous Presidents have made with leaders of other nations.

Congress can also pass resolutions stating that unlawful Signing Statements by Pres. Bush should be immediately rescinded by Pres. Obama because the Constitution established three equal branches of government, not a unitary Presidency; Executive privilege has limits.

This short book seeks to describe every statute, agreement, signing statement, recent status of forces agreement, and department or commission regulation that violates basic U.S. law and can be immediately repealed, amended, or unfunded. It also cites "laws" upheld by the U.S. Supreme Court that can now be repealed or amended by the new Congress.

Each "law" is described as follows:

- Name of Bush-Cheney "law."[5]
- Citation.
- Who is hurt by this "law" in the U.S. or anywhere in the world.
- Brief description of what the "law" provides.
- List of provisions of the U.S. Constitution and ratified treaties that this Bush-Cheney "law" ignores or violates.[6]
- Citation to any bill proposed in the House or Senate to amend or repeal this "law" as of August 1, 2008.
- Steps Congress can take immediately.

The Bush-Cheney "laws" to include were found in the voting records of leading Congress members, in the charges against Bush and Cheney in the book by Rep. Conyers and Holtzman,[7] in the impeachment resolutions submitted to the House Judiciary Committee by Rep. Dennis Kucinich, in headline news on the radio and TV, in newspapers and magazines, and in newsletters of many NonGovernmental Organizations.

Call for Help

While we worked very hard to make this list complete and accurate as of the end of the 110th Congressional session and the close of the 2007-2008 Supreme Court term, please send us any additions!

We thank all of the people who sent articles and websites for this tool kit. We have listed everyone who sent write-ups. Liz Troutman, 3L at U. of North Carolina School of Law, our Haywood Burns National Lawyers Guild intern; Twila Flores, '08 graduate of New College School of Law, our MCLI Summer Intern; John Tomasek, our pre-law intern, all worked all summer on this Tool Kit. Corrie Willis and Jennifer Smith, MCLI staff, worked on corrections and organizing the book. J. Richard Challacombe did a masterful job of formatting. Evan Waldinger, Illustrator and friend of MCLI, designed the cover. All of their contributions were invaluable. Board member Abbot Foote played his role as community steward. I did the editing and outlining and tried to catch all errors.

-- Ann Fagan Ginger, Editor

NOTE (December 20, 2008): Presidential and Congressional bailouts of Fanny Mae, Freddy Mac and American International Group, and later of General Motors and Chrysler, were added to the first edition, issued in Sept. 2008. See new pages 152-158. We welcome your input for the next edition.

---

[1] Bush-Cheney tied together dozens of statutes and regulations and enacted them into the so-called USA PATRIOT Act. Should the Progressive Caucus propose one massive act in the new Congress to form the acronym: T H E R E S T O R I N G D E M O C R A C Y ACT OF 2009, starting with

T: The USA Patriot Act and Patriot Improvement and Reauthorization Act of 2005 Repeal Act of 2009

H: Homeland Security Act Repeal Act of 2009

E: Excess Profits Tax Repeal Act Repealed in 2009

R: Repeal REAL ID Act

E: Enact Endangered Species Strengthing Act of 2009 ...

[2] John C. Conyers & Elizabeth Holtzman, "The Constitution In Crisis: The High Crimes of the Bush Administration and a Blueprint for Impeachment" (Skyhorse Publishing, April 2007)

[3] S. 3731, 109th Congress.

[4] These are Agreements, not treaties, never approved by Congress.

[5] A few of the headings do not follow this style because they describe good laws that are being badly enforced, or not being enforced at all.

[6] Brief quotations from these laws are on the following pages. The full text of relevant provisions of each law mentioned is in the Appendix.

[7] Op. cit. note 2.

TEXT OF THE LAW in U.S. Constitution, Statutes and Treaties (excerpts)

U. S. Constitution:

General Welfare Clause, Art. I, §8, cl. 1: "The Congress shall have Power...to provide for the...general Welfare of the United States."

Art. I, §9, cl. 2.: "The Privilege of the Writ of Habeas Corpus shall not be suspended, unless when in Cases of Rebellion or Invasion the public Safety may require it."

First Amendment: "Congress shall make no law...abridging the freedom of speech, or of the press; or the right of the people peaceably to assemble and to petition the Government for a redress of grievances."

Fourth Amendment: "The right of the people to be secure in their persons, houses, papers, and effects, against unreasonable searches and seizures, shall not be violated, and no Warrants shall issue, but upon probable cause, supported by Oath or affirmation, and particularly describing the place to be searched, and the persons or things to be seized."

Fifth Amendment: "No person shall be held to answer for a capital, or otherwise infamous crime, unless on...indictment of a Grand Jury, except in cases arising in the land or naval forces,...in time of War or public danger;... nor be deprived of life, liberty, or property, without due process of law..."

Ninth Amendment: "The enumeration in the Constitution, of certain rights, shall not be construed to deny...others retained by the people."

Tenth Amendment: "The powers not delegated to the United States by the Constitution, nor prohibited by it to the States, are reserved to the States respectively, or to the people."

U.S. Statutes:

War Crimes Act of 1996, 18 U.S.C. Part I, Ch. 118, §2441: "(a) Offense.—Whoever, whether inside or outside the United States, commits a war crime,...shall be fined...or imprisoned for life or any term of years ...(c) ...the term "war crime" means any conduct—(1) defined as a grave breach in any of the international conventions signed at Geneva 12 August 1949, or any protocol to such convention to which the United States is a party;..."

Anti-Torture Statute. 18 U.S.C. Part I, Ch. 113C, §2340(1): "'torture' means an act committed by a person acting under the color of law specifically intended to inflict severe physical or mental pain or suffering (other than pain or suffering incident to lawful sanctions) upon another person within his custody or physical control;..."

U. N. Charter:

Preamble: "We the Peoples of the United Nations Determined...to reaffirm faith in fundamental human rights, in the dignity and worth of the human person, in the equal rights of men and women and of nations large and small..."

Art. 2(4): "All Members shall refrain in their international relations from the threat or use of force against the territorial integrity or political independence of any state, or in any other manner inconsistent with the Purposes of the United Nations."

Art. 55: "With a view to the creation of conditions of stability and well-being which are necessary for peaceful and friendly relations among nations...,"

Geneva Conventions:

Geneva Convention (Relative to the Treatment of Prisoners of War), Art. 118, Aug. 12, 1949, 6 U.S.T. 3316: "In the case of armed conflict not of an international character...each party to the conflict shall be bound to apply, as a minimum,...: (1)...the following acts are and shall remain prohibited at any time and in any place whatsoever...:(a) Violence to life and person, in particular murder,... mutilation, cruel treatment and torture;...(c) outrages upon personal dignity,...humiliating and degrading treatment;..."

International Covenant on Civil and Political Rights (ICCPR):

Preamble: "...recognition of the inherent dignity and of the equal and inalienable rights of all members of the human family is the foundation of freedom, justice and peace in the world..."

Art. 2(1): "Each State Party to the present Covenant undertakes to respect and to ensure to all individuals within its territory and subject to its jurisdiction the rights recognized in the present Covenant, without distinction of any kind, such as race, colour, sex, language, religion, political or other opinion, national or social origin, property, birth or other status."

Art. 7: "No one shall be subjected to torture or to cruel, inhuman or degrading treatment or punishment..." Everyone has the right to liberty and security of person. No one shall be subjected to arbitrary arrest or detention. No one shall be deprived of his liberty except... and in accordance with...law."

Art. 9 (1): "Everyone has the right to liberty and security of person."

Art. 9(2): "Anyone who is arrested shall be informed, at the time of arrest, of the reasons...and shall be promptly informed of any charges against him."

Art. 9(3): "Anyone arrested or detained on a criminal charge shall be brought promptly before a judge or other officer authorized by law...and shall be entitled to trial within a reasonable time or to release..."

Art. 9(4): "Anyone who is deprived of his liberty by arrest or detention shall be entitled to take proceedings before a court,...[that] may decide without delay on the lawfulness of his detention and order his release if the detention is not lawful."

Art. 10(1): "All persons deprived of their liberty shall be treated with humanity and respect for the inherent dignity of the human person."

Art. 14(3): "In the determination of any criminal charge...,
everyone shall be entitled to the following minimum guarantees, in full equality: (a) to be informed promptly and in a language which he understands of the nature and cause of the charge...; (b) to have adequate time and facilities for the preparation of his defence and to communicate with counsel of his own choosing; (c) to be tried without undue delay; (d) to be tried in his presence, and to defend himself in person or through legal assistance of his own choosing; ...and to have legal assistance assigned..., in any case where the interests of justice so require; and without payment by him... if he does not have sufficient means...; (e)...have examined, the witnesses against him

6

and to obtain the attendance and examination of witnesses on his behalf ...; (f) to have the free assistance of an interpreter if [needed]; (g) Not to be compelled to testify against himself..."

Art. 16(1): "Everyone shall have the right to recognition everywhere as a person before the law."

Art. 22(1): "Everyone shall have the right to freedom of association..., including the right to form and join trade unions for the protection of his interests."

Art. 23(1): "The family is the natural and fundamental group unit of society and is entitled to protection by society and the State."

Art. 24(1): "Every child shall have, without any discrimination as to race, colour, sex, language, religion, national or social origin, property or birth, the right to such measures of protection as are required by his status as a minor, on the part of his family, society and the State."

Convention Against Torture and Other Cruel, Inhuman or Degrading Treatment or Punishment (ICAT):

Art. 2(1): "Each State Party shall take effective legislative, administrative, judicial or other measures to prevent acts of torture in any territory under its jurisdiction."

Art. 2(2): "No exceptional circumstance whatsoever, whether a state of war or a threat of war, internal political instability or any other public emergency, may be invoked as a justification for torture."

Art. 3(1): "No State Party shall expel, return or extradite a person to another state where there are substantial grounds for believing that he would be in danger of being subjected to torture."

Art. 3(2): "...the competent authorities shall take into account all relevant considerations including...the existence...of a consistent pattern of gross, flagrent or mass violations of human rights."

Art. 5(1): "Each State party shall take such measures as may be necessary to establish its jurisdiction over the offenses...in article 4...: (a) When the offences are committed in any territory under its jurisdiction or on board a ship or aircraft registered in that State; (b) When the alleged offender is a national of that state; (c) When the victim is a national of that State ..."

Art. 11: "Each State Party shall keep under systematic review interrogation rules,..., methods and practices as well as arrangements for the custody and treatment of persons subjected to any form of arrest, detention or imprisonment in any territory under its jurisdiction, with a view to preventing any cases of torture."

Art. 16(1): "Each State Party shall undertake to prevent in any territory under its jurisdiction other acts of cruel, inhuman or degrading treatment or punishment...when such acts are committed by or at the instigation of or with the...acquiescence of a public official ...""

International Convention on the Elimination of all Forms of Racial Discrimination:

Art. 2, 1: "States Parties condemn racial discrimination and undertake to pursue by all appropriate means and without delay a policy of eliminating racial discrimination in all its forms and promoting understanding among all races, and, to this end: (a) Each State Party undertakes to engage in no act or practice of racial discrimination against persons, groups of persons or institutions and to en sure that all public authorities and public institutions, national and local, shall act in conformity with this obligation; (b) Each State Party undertakes not to sponsor, defend or support racial discrimination by any persons or organizations; (c) Each State Party shall take effective measures to review governmental, national and local policies, and to amend, rescind or nullify any laws and regulations which have the effect of creating or perpetuating racial discrimination wherever it exists; (d) Each State Party shall prohibit and bring to an end, by all appropriate means, including legislation as required by circumstances, racial discrimination by any persons, group or organization; (e) Each State Party undertakes to encourage, where appropriate, integrationist multiracial organizations and movements and other means of eliminating barriers between races, and to discourage anything which tends to strengthen racial division."

Art. 2, 2: "States Parties shall, when the circumstances so warrant, take, in the social, economic, cultural and other fields, special and concrete measures to ensure the adequate development and protection of certain racial groups or individuals belonging to them, for the purpose of guaranteeing them the full and equal enjoyment of human rights and fundamental freedoms. These measures shall in no case entail as a consequence the maintenance of unequal or separate rights for different racial groups after the objectives for which they were taken have been achieved."

Art. 5: "In compliance with the fundamental obligations laid down in article 2..., States Parties undertake to prohibit and to eliminate racial discrimination in all its forms and to guarantee the right of everyone, without discrimination as to race, colour, or national or ethnic origin, to equality before the law,...(e) Economic, social and cultural rights, in particular:...(iv) The right to public health, medical care, social security and social service;..."

AGRICULTURE

Bush "Law": Sewage disposal permits issued for Concentrated Animal Feed Operations (CAFOSs)

Citation: Clean Water Act (CWA), 33 U.S.C. §§1251, and 33 U.S.C. §1345(a), et seq.

Who is hurt by this "law": CAFOs are large corporate farms that keep animals in high concentrations and produce over 160 volatile organic compounds, such as ammonia and hydrogen sulfide, that cause irritation to human eyes and respiratory systems and decrease property values.[1] In 2005, the U.S. 2nd Circuit Court of Appeals ordered the Environmental Protection Agency (EPA) to implement changes to improve water quality from CAFOs, but the EPA has not done so.[2] In 2008, one of these "factory farms" dumped 750,000 gallons of untreated swine manure in Bureau Creek, Illinois, which resulted in a massive fish kill.[3]

What the "law" provides: CAFOs have to apply for National Pollutant Discharge Elimination System (NPDES) permits through the EPA that allow disposal of sewage sludge. "[W]here the disposal of sewage sludge resulting from the operation of a treatment works ...would result in any pollutant from such sewage entering the navigable waters, such disposal is prohibited except in accordance with a permit issued by the Administrator under section 1342 of this title." Problems arise because CAFOs must admit that they are a source of sewage when they apply for the permit, but if they don't, they continue to dispose of their sewage into water supplies.

What the "law" ignores: U.S. Constitution, Art. 1, §8, cl. 1: "The Congress shall have Power to...provide for the...general Welfare ..."

Office of the Inspector General reports on Region III in 2005: recommending "(a) discontinuing the use of permit language that weakens permits;...and (c) require States to prepare Clean Water Act §106 work plans that target the issuance of specific permits and withhold funds when these permits are not renewed timely."[4]

What Congress can do: Congress can pass **S. 1407**: Concentrated Livestock Existing Alongside Nature Act (introduced 7/15/2003); sponsored by Sen. John Edwards (D-NC).

See also: www.sierraclub.org/factoryfarms

[1] http://www.defenders.org (6/5/08).

[2] http://www.bloomingtonalternative.com/node/8336 (6/5/08).

[3] http://www.week.com/news/local/18942419.html (6/5/08).

[4] www.epa.gov/oigearth/reports/2005/20041029-2005-S-00002.pdf Congressionally Requested Review of EPA Region 3's Oversight of State National Pollutant Discharge Elimination System Permit Programs, report no. 2005-S-00002 (Oct. 29, 2004).

ANTI-TRUST

Bush "Law": Federal Communications Commission Cross-Ownership Rules Relaxed

Citation: Report and Order FCC 07-216 amending 47 C.F.R. §73.3555.

Who is hurt by this "law": Everyone in the U.S. who watches television, reads newspapers, listens to the radio, or accesses the internet is hurt by cross-media mergers. Cross-media mergers occur when owners of a television station purchases a newspaper. These cross-media mergers reduce the diversity of ownership of media outlets that reduces the diversity of opinions and viewpoints that are available to the general public and hinders democracy. According to Florida Public Interest Research Group, this consolidation of the media results in Miami having a homogenous media and increases the concentration of media outlets to levels near the monopoly limits.[1]

What the "law" provides: In December 2007, the FCC voted 3-2 (GOP for, Dems against) to get rid of a 32 year old ban on cross-ownership of broadcasters and newspapers within the same market.[2] This means that television stations and radio stations are now permitted to purchase newspapers within the same local market, thereby consolidating media sources.[3]

What the "law" ignores:

U.S. Constitution, First Amendment.

Sherman Antitrust Act, §2: "Every person who shall monopolize, or attempt... to monopolize any part of the...commerce among the several States,...shall be...guilty of a felony."

ICCPR, Art. 19 (2).

Bills proposed to repeal the "law":

S.J. Res. 28: A joint resolution disapproving the rule submitted by the FCC broadcast media ownership (passed Senate 5/15/08); sponsored by Sen. Byron Dorgan (D-ND).

Identical **H.J. Res. 79**: (introduced 3/13/08); sponsored by Rep. Jay Inslee (D-WA) with 31 cosponsors.

What Congress can do: In 2009, Congressmembers can reintroduce and pass S.J. Res. 28 and H.J. Res. 79 if they do not become law late in 2008.

See also: Stopbigmedia.com

---

[1] Florida PIRG, *How Bigger Media Will Hurt Florida: A Report on Florida Media Markets and the Impact of Newspaper/TV Cross-Ownership Mergers*, October 2006.

[2] John Eggerton, *FCC Loosens Newspaper-Broadcast Cross-Ownership Limits, Broadcasting & Cable,* December 18, 2007.

[3] Federal Communications Agency, *FCC's Review of the Broadcast Ownership Rules,* http://www.fcc.gov/cgb/consumerfacts/reviewrules.pdf, (6/7/08).

BUDGET

Bush Law: Labor, HHS, Education Appropriations Act of 2006

Citation: Departments of Labor, Health & Human Services, and Education, & Related Agencies Appropriations Act of 2006 [H.R. 3010]

Who is hurt by this law:

Community-Based Job Training programs and their participants.

Centers for Medicare and Medicaid and their users.

Agriculture programs and their participants.

Food stamp programs and their participants.

And everyone is hurt who supports assistance to those U.S. residents seeking to move forward with their lives.

What the law provides: In his FY 2006 Budget Resolution, Bush proposed cuts in funding and size of programs and services. Congress implemented many of these cuts. LHEAA includes: "Of the funds provided under this heading in division F of Public Law 108-447 for Community-Based Job Training Grants, $125,000,000 is rescinded...in Public Law 108-7 to carry out section 173(a)(4)(A) of the Workforce Investment Act of 1998, $20,000,000 are rescinded... the amounts specified under such heading for the Centers for Medicare and Medicaid Services System Revitalization be reduced by the Secretary."

This led to $10 billion in cuts from the Medicaid Program, $3 billion from agriculture and food-stamp programs, $125 million from job training programs[1].

Bush then issued his "Statement of Administration Policy": the President is "extremely pleased that the Committee...reported a fiscally responsible bill that eliminates nearly half the programs the President proposed for termination and reduces a number of others."[3]

See also: Department of Defense (DOD) Budget for War on Iraq

What the law ignores:

U.S. Constitution, General Welfare Clause, Art. 1, §8, cl. 1.

14

U.S. Constitution, Ninth Amendment.
ICCPR, Art. 23, §1: re the family.
ICCPR, Art. 24, §2: re rights of the child.

What Congress can do: In 2009, Congress can adopt a resolution that the precedent established by the coupling of the Budget Resolution and the Departments of Labor, Health and Human Services, and Education, and Related Agencies Appropriations Act FY 2006 will be reversed.

---

[1] "Senate Report 109-103 – Departments of Labor, Health and Human Services, and Education, and Related Agencies Appropriation Bill, 2006." The Library of Congress, THOMAS. 2006. Retrieved June 12, 2008 from: http://thomas.loc.gov/cgi-bin/cpquery/?&dbname=cp109&sid=cp1092kIP g&refer=&r_n=sr103.109&item=&sel=TOC_11437&

[2] "House Ignores Bush Medicare, Medicaid Cuts in Passing Budget Resolutions." Senior Citizen Politics. Seniorjournal.com. May 18, 2006. Retrieved on June 14, 2006 from <http://seniorjournal.com/NEWS/ Politics/6-05-18-HouseIgnores.htm>.

[3] "Statement of Administration Policy: H.R. 3010...Appropriations Bill, FY 2006." Executive Office of the President: Office of Management and Budget. June 23, 2005. Retrieved on June 13, 2008 from: http:// www.whitehouse.gov/omb/legislative/sap/109-1/hr3010sap-h.pdf

Bush Budget for Military Aid for Israel Ignoring Existing Law

Citation: Human Rights and Security Assistance Act of 1974, 22 U.S.C.A. ¶ 2304

Who is hurt by Bush miliary aid to Israel: After Israeli-Palestine cease fire agreement expired Dec. 19, 2008, both sides fired rockets. In Gaza, Israel hurled U.S.-made bombs at civilians from U.S. military planes bought with U.S. funding.

What the "law" ignores: The Human Rights and Security Assistance Act Secion (a)(2): "No security assistance may be provided to any country the government of which engages in a consistent pattern of gross violations of internationnally recognized human rights."

United Nations Charter, Art. 2(4): "All members shall refrain in their international relations from the threat or use of force against the territorial integrity or political independence of any state, or ... inconsistent with the Purposes of the United Nations."

U.N. Secretary General Ban Ki-moon Dec. 26. 2008: Hamas and U.S. bombs used by Israel violate U.N. Charter.

DEATH PENALTY

Bush "Law": National Application of Federal Capital Sentencing Laws

Citation: United States Attorney Manual, Title 9, §§10.010- 10.190

Who is hurt by this "law:" Marcia Coyle of the *National Law Journal* reports that the Federal Government authorized 180 prosecutions seeking the death penalty in the 1990s and 240 since 2000. Of these, 57 individuals received the death penalty, 32 under the Bush administration and the Department of Justice's (DOJ) new protocol.[1]

The Tenth Amendment of the U.S. Constitution provides that "powers not delegated to the United States...are reserved to the States respectively...," and established state's police powers to be exercised exclusively by state governments. The DOJ, charged with "control over federal law enforcement"[2], is permitted to pursue the death penalty as punishment for those crimes enumerated in the Federal Death Penalty Act of 1994 and the Anti-Drug Abuse Act of 1988. This enumeration of crimes punishable by death, coupled with the directions in the U. S. Attorney Manual, expose individuals under the jurisdiction of the states to cruel and unusual punishment as imposed by the Federal government.

What the "law" provides: In June 2001, the Bush Administration revised the DOJ Death Penalty protocol to create nationwide uniformity of its application,[3] regardless of a state's policy on the death penalty, and a less transparent process.[4] The new protocol includes:

"When concurrent jurisdiction exists with a State or local government, a Federal indictment for an offense subject to the death penalty generally should be obtained only when the Federal interest in the prosecution is more substantial than the interests of the State or local authorities."[5]

16

"The decision-making process preliminary to the Attorney General's final decision is confidential. Information concerning the deliberative process may only be disclosed within the Department... as necessary to assist the review and decision-making. In no event may the information identified in this paragraph be disclosed outside the Department...without prior approval of the Attorney General."[6]

"The review of cases under this Chapter culminates in a decision to seek, or not to seek, the death penalty against an individual defendant. Each such decision must be based upon the facts and law applicable to the case and be set within a framework of consistent and even-handed national application of Federal capital sentencing laws."[7]

David Bruck, a South Carolina attorney with the Death Penalty Resource Counsel Project, says "It appears to be a strategy to ensure that the federal death penalty is widely applied throughout the country without regard to the attitudes and beliefs and policies of the people in each state."

What the "law" ignores:

U.S. Constitution, Eighth Amendment: "Excessive bail shall not be required,...nor cruel and unusual punishments inflicted."

U.S. Constitution, Tenth Amendment: "The powers not delegated to the United States by the Constitution, nor prohibited by it to the States, are reserved to the States respectively, or to the people."

ICCPR, Art. 6, §§1-6.

ICCPR, Art. 14, §5.

What Congress can do: In 2009, Congress can respond to the increasing public disapproval of the death penalty,[9] and take into account that such eminent Supreme Court Justices as Marshall and Brennan declared in their decisions in *Furman v. Georgia* (1972) that "The punishment of death is therefore 'cruel and unusual'"[10] and therefore in violation of the Eighth Amendment. Congress can ensure that the issue of the death penalty is left to the states, by narrowing those federal crimes which can be punished by death, or get rid of the death penalty as a punishment for federal crimes altogether.

---

[1] "The Federal Death Penalty." Death Penalty Information Center. 2008. Retrieved on July 28, 2008 from <http://www.deathpenaltyinfo.org/article.php?did=147&scid=>.

[2] "Statutory Authority." Department of Justice. www.usdoj.gov. Retrieved on July 29, 2008 from < http://www.usdoj.gov/02organizations/>.

[3] David Bruck. "Memorandum- 2007 Revisions to DOJ Death Penalty Provisions." July 1, 2007. www.capdefnet.org. Retrieved on July 28, 2008 from <http://www.capdefnet.org/pdf_library/Summary_of_changes_in_2007_DOJ_death_penalty_protocol.pdf>.

[4] Supra note 3.

[5] "United States Attorneys Manual." Department of Justice. Title 9-10.090. Retrieved on July 28, 2008 from <http://www.usdoj.gov/usao/eousa/foia_reading_room/usam/title9/ 10mcrm.htm#9-10.010>.

[6] "United States Attorneys Manual." Department of Justice. Title 9-10.040. Retrieved on July 28, 2008 from <http://www.usdoj.gov/usao/eousa/foia_reading_room/usam/title9/ 10mcrm.htm#9-10.010>.

[7] "United States Attorneys Manual." Department of Justice. Title 9-10.030. Retrieved on July 28, 2008 from <http://www.usdoj.gov/usao/eousa/foia_reading_room/usam/title9/ 10mcrm.htm#9-10.010>.

[8] Shelley Murphy. "Death Penalty foes rap Ashcroft." The Boston Globe. September 20, 2003. Retrieved on July 28, 2008 from <http://www.boston.com/news/local/articles /2003/09/20/death_penalty_foes_rap_ashcroft?mode=PF>.

[9] "Facts About the Death Penalty." Death Penalty Information Center. July 16, 2008. www.deathpenaltyinfo.org. Retrieved on July 29, 2008 from <<http://www.deathpenaltyinfo.org/FactSheet.pdf>.

[10] 408 U.S. 238; 92 S. Ct. 2726; 33 L. Ed. 2d 346; 1972 U.S. LEXIS 169. Retrieved on July 28, 2008 from <http://supreme.justia.com/us/408/238/case.html>.

DEPARTMENT OF HOMELAND SECURITY

Homeland Security Presidential Directive 20

Uniting and Strengthening America by Providing Appropriate Tools Required to Intercept and Obstruct Terrorism Act of 2001 (USA PATRIOT Act)

Presidential authority to use PATRIOT Act powers in secret without critical review mandated by Congress

Homeland Security Act of 2002 (HSA)

Statement on Signing the Intelligence Reform and Terrorism Prevention Act of 2004

Real ID Act of 2005

Mismanagement of Hurricanes Katrina and Rita Relief Efforts

Animal Enterprise Terrorism Act of 2006 (AETA)

Failure to Appoint Privacy and Civil Liberties Oversight Board

Foreign Intelligence Surveillance Act (FISA) Amendments Act of 2008

Violent Radicalization and Homegrown Terrorism Prevention Act of 2007

Bush "Law": Homeland Security Presidential Directive 20

Citation: National Security Presidential Directive 51 (NSPD-51), May 9, 2007[1]

Who is hurt by this "law": In case of a national emergency, every person in the U.S. will be hurt by this Directive because it gives the President and the executive branch the authority to essentially take over the entire government, calling it the creation of an "enduring constitutional government." If an "emergency" were to be declared

19

during an election, for example, and the President invoked NSPD-51, Pres. Bush could suspend the election indefinitely and retain executive power.[2]

What the "law" provides: The Directive says that if there is a national emergency, "continuity of government" will be maintained by establishing the National Continuity Coordinator (NCC) under the President. Definition (e) of the Directive defines "Enduring Constitutional Government" as "a cooperative effort among the executive, legislative, and judicial branches of the Federal Government, coordinated by the President, as a matter of comity with respect to the legislative and judicial branches and with proper respect for the constitutional separation of powers among the branches, to preserve the constitutional framework under which the Nation is governed and the capability of all three branches of government to execute constitutional responsibilities and provide for orderly succession, appropriate transition of leadership, and interoperability and support of the National Essential Functions during a catastrophic emergency."

The definition of "catastrophic emergency" is "any incident, regardless of location that results in extraordinary levels of mass casualties, damage, or disruption severely affecting the U.S. population, infrastructure, environment, economy, or government functions;"

Implementation Action (6) says, "[t]he President shall lead the activities of the Federal Government for ensuring constitutional government. In order to advise and assist the President in that function, the Assistant to the President for Homeland Security and Counterterrorism (APHS/DT) is hereby designated as the National Continuity Coordinator. The National Continuity Coordinator, in coordination with the Assistant to the President for National Security Affairs (APNSA), without exercising directive authority, shall coordinate the development and implementation of continuity policy for executive departments and agencies..."

What the "law" ignores:
  U.S. Constitution, Separation of Powers.
  U.S. Constitution, General Welfare Clause, Art. I, §8, cl. 1.
  U.S. Constitution, Tenth Amendment.
  U.N. Charter, Preamble.
  U.N. Charter, Art. 55 & 56.

20

ICCPR, Preamble.
ICCPR, Art. 2(1).
ICAT, Art. 2(2).
ICAT, Art. 16(1).

What Congress can do: In 2009, Congressmembers can introduce and pass legislation specifically rejecting National Security Directive 51.

See also: Matthew Rothschild, *Bush Anoints Himself as the Insurer of Constitutional Government in Emergency, The Progressive,* May 20, 2007, http://www.progressive.org (8/4/08).

---

[1] http://www.whitehouse.gov/news/releases/2007/05/20070509-12.html, (8/4/08).
[2] Ron Rosenbaum, *Who Will Run the Country After the Next 9/11?, Slate Magazine,* Oct. 19, 2007, http://www.slate.com/id/2176185/, (8/4/08).

Bush Law: Uniting and Strengthening America by Providing Appropriate Tools Required to Intercept and Obstruct Terrorism Act of 2001 (USA PATRIOT Act)

Citation: Public Law 107-56, 115 Stat. 272.

Who has been hurt by this law: Because of the secrecy surrounding enforcement of the PATRIOT Act, many abuses caused by this law have not yet been reported. Two have been reported.

In 2004, the FBI, using its expanded powers under the Act, arrested and imprisoned Brandon Mayfield, an attorney from Oregon, because the FBI thought he was involved in the 2004 terrorist attacks on trains in Madrid. Mayfield sued the government, which eventually settled the case and issued an apology.[1]

The Department of Homeland Security also revoked the visa of Tariq Ramadan, a Muslim intellectual who denounces the use of violence in the name of Islam. DHS said non-citizens may be excluded from the country if they use their position of prominence to endorse terrorist activity, even if that person does not support terrorist activity himself.[2] Any other non-citizen in a "position of prominence" could be targeted if they discuss their political beliefs.

What the law provides:

§206: permits secret intelligence wiretap orders that need not specify in advance the person or place to be tapped.

§213: authorizes the use of so-called "sneak and peek" search warrants that permit the authorities to break into a home or place of business, search belongings and computers, seize property and leave without notifying the target for an indefinite period of time.

§215: lets the FBI obtain orders from a top-secret "intelligence court" for the production of "any tangible things." The FBI need not have any evidence that the target of the order is engaged in espionage or terrorist activity, and need only assert that the information sought is relevant to an ongoing investigation. The "intelligence court" judge has no statutory authority to question this assertion, and must grant the order if it is requested. Once issued, the recipient of the order cannot tell anyone about the order except those necessary for its execution.

§505: removed the requirement that there be some individual suspicion that the records seized using "national security letters" pertain to a foreign spy or terrorist. These national security letters can be used to obtain sensitive financial and credit records and are not reviewed by a judge in advance of their execution.

§802: created a legal definition of "domestic terrorism" that is not linked to any particular criminal offense and can therefore be used by overzealous prosecutors to trigger highly invasive investigations of political activists on the right or the left.

The Act has a four-year sunset provision. In 2005, after a very contentious battle, it was filibustered in December, then passed in March 2006 with a final vote in the Senate of 95-4, with one not voting, and in the House, 280-138, with 14 not voting. Several sections of the Act are due to sunset in 2009.

The efforts to make almost all of the PATRIOT Act permanent with few substantive reforms was met by strong resistance from an unlikely coalition across the political spectrum.

What the law ignores:
U.S. Constitution, First Amendment.
U.S. Constitution, Fourth Amendment.
U.S. Constitution, Fifth Amendment.
U.S. Constitution, Ninth Amendment.
U.N. Charter, Articles 55 and 56.
International Covenant on Civil and Political Rights (ICCPR), Preamble.

ICCPR, Art. 17: "(1) No one shall be subject to arbitrary or unlawful interference with his privacy, family, or correspondence, nor to unlawful attacks on his honour and reputation. (2) Everyone has the right to the protection of the law against such interference or attacks."

What Congress can do: Congressmembers can repeal all of the above sections and reject any proposal to remove the sunset from the sections in 2009.

See also: American Civil Liberties Union, http://action.aclu.org/reformthepatriotact/

Contributor: ACLU Washington Legislative Office

---

[1] Dan Eggen, *U.S. Settles Suit Filed by Ore. Lawyer, Washington Post,* 11/30/2006.

[2] American Civil Liberties Union, http://action.aclu.org/reformthepatriotact/facts.html#one, (7/2/08).

Bush "Law": Presidential authority to use PATRIOT Act powers in secret without critical review mandated by Congress

Citation: Statement on Signing USA PATRIOT Improvement and Reauthorization Act of 2005, 42 Weekly Comp Pres. Doc. 425 (Mar. 9, 2006)

What the "law" provides: The executive branch shall construe the provisions of H.R. 3199 that call for furnishing information to entities outside the executive branch, such as sections 106A and 119, "in a manner consistent with the President's constitutional authority to supervise the unitary executive branch and to withhold information the disclosure of which could impair foreign relations, national security, the deliberative processes of the Executive, or the performance of the Executive's constitutional duties."

Who is hurt by this "law": Congressmembers who first quickly voted for the PATRIOT Act after 9/11, then discovered the violations of constitutional rights committed under that Act and voted in 2005 to reauthorize some measures but also required the Inspector General for the Department of Justice to conduct audits of the use of these powers, consider their efficacy, and report back to Congress. People in the U. S. who believe in Democracy set forth in the Constitution are also hurt.

What the "law" ignores:

USA PATRIOT Improvement and Reauthorization Act of 2005, Pub. L. No. 109-177, §§ 106A, 119, 120 Stat. 192, 200-02, 219-21 (2006)

U.S. Constitution, Art. II, Sec. 3, requiring that the President "shall take Care that the Laws be faithfully executed."

U.S. Constitution, Art. I, Sec. 7, Cl. 2, requiring the President to either approve and sign a bill or return it to Congress for consideration of an override of his veto.

See also Clinton v. City of New York, 524 U.S. 417 (1998) (invalidating the line-item veto).

What Congress can do: In 2009, Congress can: (1) act on Sen. Arlen Specter's (R-PA) legislation (first proposed in 2006 as the Presidential Signing Statements Act, S. 3731, 109th Cong.) that would instruct the federal courts to disregard signing statements and provide standing to Members of Congress who wish to challenge such statements in court; (2) pass legislation clarifying that signing statements, including this one, do not alter the requirements of the law; (3) refuse to confirm any nominees for office until it is clear that they understands that their duty is to the law as passed by Congress and signed by the President, without regard to signing statements or other anti-democratic maneuvers.

Contributor: Prof. Zachary Wolfe, George Washington University

Bush Law: Homeland Security Act of 2002 (HSA)

Citation: Public Law 107-296, 116 Stat. 2135 (2002).

Who is hurt by this law: Anyone in the United States or wishing to come to the U.S. or wishing to have contact with anyone in the U. S. is hurt by the HSA because the Act authorizes collection of information permitting sweeping invasions of privacy and puts civil liberties at risk.

The enormous national database with information on people in the U.S. is susceptible to abuse. In one instance, an employee of the Department of Commerce—now under the Department of Homeland Security (DHS)—with access to the database used it to stalk his ex-girlfriend.[1] Even more widespread and egregious abuses are possible. In 2006, the DHS gave the Pentagon information on anti-war protesters at University of California campuses, even though those protestors were not doing anything illegal. "Homeland Security was created to protect the American people from terrorist activities – not monitor political dissent on college campuses," according to Mark Schlosberg of the ACLU of Northern California[2] (*See also*: Real ID Act – General; USA PATRIOT Act; FISA).

U.S. Customs and Border Protection, also under the umbrella of the DHS, has been targeting Arab and Muslim citizens and travelers at airports and other ports of entry for searches and questioning simply on the basis of their ethnicity and appearance, which is racial profiling.[3] A program introduced in 2002 known as the National Security Entry-Exit Registration System (NSEERS) is purportedly an anti-terrorism measure but actually discriminates based on nation of origin. It requires male visitors to the U.S. from 25 Arab and Muslim countries and North Korea to be fingerprinted, photographed and questioned by immigration authorities. Around 84,000 Arabs and Muslims voluntarily registered. Afterwards, about 14,000 were put through deportation hearings, but none were charged with terrorism-related crimes, according to the American-Arab Anti-Discrimination Committee.[4]

The Act reorganized the U.S. Immigration and Naturalization Service and created the U.S. Immigration and Customs Enforcement, which answers to DHS. The impact of this reorganization is that the migration of people and the importation of all goods—whether coconuts or weapons—are all managed by the same agency. Putting people and goods in the same category is degrading towards immigrants and non-immigrants in the U.S. who wish to enter or remain in the U.S. (See also: Funding and Administrative Support for Massive Immigration Raids: Homeland Security Act of 2002).

What the law provides: The Homeland Security Act was passed by Congress at Pres. Bush's request in the wake of 9/11 and created a new cabinet position and a new executive agency: the Department of Homeland Security. This Act initiated the largest federal government reorganization since creation of the Department of Defense (DoD) in 1947. The Act provides that the following agencies now fall under the authority of DHS: U.S. Immigration & Customs Enforcement, Federal Emergency Management Agency, Transportation Security Administration, U.S. Customs & Border Protection, U.S. Citizenship and Immigration Services, U.S. Coast Guard, U.S. Secret Service and other sub-departments of various agencies. The primary goals of DHS are to "(A) prevent terrorist attacks within the [U.S.]; (B) reduce the vulnerability of the [U.S.] to terrorism; and (C) minimize the damage, and assist in the recovery, from terrorist attacks..."[5]

Sec. 203 provides that "[t]he Secretary shall have access to all reports, assessments, and analytical information relating to threats of terrorism in the United States...and to all information concerning infrastructure or other vulnerabilities of the United States to terrorism...." This provision has been used to justify increased surveillance and loss of privacy of people in the U.S.

What the law ignores:
  U.S. Constitution, General Welfare Clause, Art. I, §8, cl. 1.
  U.S. Constitution, First Amendment.
  U.S. Constitution, Fourth Amendment.
  U.S. Constitution, the privacy protections in the penumbra of the
    First and Ninth Amendments.
  U.N. Charter, Preamble.
  U.N. Charter, Art. 55 & 56.
  ICCPR, Preamble.
  ICCPR, Art. 2(1).
  ICCPR, Art. 17(1).
  ICCPR, Art. 19.
  ICCPR, Art. 22(1).
  ICCPR, Art. 26.
  ICAT, Art. 2(2).
  ICAT, Art. 16(1).
  ICERD, Art. 5.
  ICERD, Art. 2(1)

What Congress can do: In 2009, Congressmembers can:
  Repeal the Homeland Security Act of 2002;
  Repeal subsequent legislation that has a similar impact as the
    HSA, e.g. REAL ID Act, USA PATRIOT Act, and FISA.
See also: William Safire, *You Are a Suspect, New York Times,* Nov. 14, 2002.

---

[1] Sharon Gaudin, *Federal Agent Indicted for Using Homeland Security Database to Stalk Girlfriend, Information Week,* Sept. 20, 2007, http://www.informationweek.com/news/management/showArticle.jhtml?articleI

D=201807903, (7/30/08).

[2] Demian Bulwa, *Terror Database Tracks UC Protests, San Francisco Chronicle,* July 19, 2006.

[3] Jim Lobe, *Racial Profiling Both Wrong and Counter-Productive, Says Amnesty,* OneWorld.net, Sept. 14, 2004, http://www.commondreams.org/cgi-bin/print.cgi?file=/headlines04/0914-03.htm, (7/30/08).

[4] *End the Shame of NSEERS, Standing FIRM,* April 18, 2007, http://fairimmigration.wordpress.com/2007/04/18/end-the-shame-of-nseers/ (7/30/08).

[5] Title I, §101(b)(1).

Bush "Law": Statement on Signing the Intelligence Reform and Terrorism Prevention Act of 2004

Citation: 40 Weekly Comp. Pres. Doc. 2993 (Dec. 17, 2004).

Who is hurt by this "law": Congress and everyone concerned about maintaining three equal branches of government are hurt by this "law." Every person is hurt by this signing statement that rejects the act of Congress ensuring oversight and protection of our privacy and civil liberties.

The Bush signing statement ignores Intelligence Reform and Terrorism Prevention Act (IRTPA) §1061 establishing within the Executive Office of the President a Privacy and Civil Liberties Oversight Board to: (1) analyze and review actions taken by the Executive branch to protect the Nation from terrorism, ensuring a balance with privacy and civil liberties protections; and (2) ensure that liberty concerns are appropriately considered in the development and implementation of laws, regulations, and policies related to efforts to protect the Nation against terrorism. Congress requires annual reports on major Board activities. IRTPA §8403 requires the Office of Government Ethics (OGE) to submit to Congress a report evaluating the financial disclosure process for executive branch employees, and requires the OGE to conduct a comprehensive review of conflict of interest laws relating to executive branch employment and report to the President and Congress on such review.

What the "law" provides: The signing statement declares "the executive branch shall construe provisions in the Act that mandate submission of information to the Congress, entities within or outside the executive branch, or the public, in a manner consistent with the President's constitutional authority to supervise the unitary executive branch and to withhold information that could impair foreign relations, national security, the deliberative processes of the Executive, or the performance of the Executive's constitutional duties...To the extent that provisions of the Act purport to require or regulate submission by executive branch officials of legislative recommendations to the Congress, the executive branch shall construe such provisions in a manner consistent with the President's constitutional authority to supervise the unitary executive branch and to submit for congressional consideration such measures as the President judges necessary and expedient."[1]

What the "law" ignores:

Intelligence Reform and Terrorism Prevention Act of 2004, Pub. L. No. 108-458, 118 Stat. 3638, 3649.

U.S. Constitution, Art. II, Sec. 3, requiring that the President "shall take Care that the Laws be faithfully executed."

U.S. Constitution, Art. I, Sec. 7, Cl. 2, requiring the President to either approve and sign a bill or return it to Congress for consideration of an override of his veto. The President has no authority to sign a bill into law but reject part of its requirements. *See also Clinton v. City of New York*, 524 U.S. 417 (1998) (invalidating the line-item veto).

ICCPR, Preamble, Art. 2, 5, and 25.

What Congress can do: In 2009, Congress can (1) act on Senator Arlen Specter's (R-PA) legislation (first proposed in 2006 as the Presidential Signing Statements Act, S. 3731, 109th Cong.) that would instruct the federal courts to disregard signing statements and provide standing to Members of Congress who wish to challenge such statements in court; (2) pass legislation clarifying that signing statements, including this one, do not alter the requirements of the law; (3) refuse to confirm any nominees for office until it is clear that they understands that their duty is to the law as passed by Congress and signed by the President, without regard to signing statements.

Contributor: Prof. Zachary Wolfe, George Washington University

---

[1]http://www.whitehouse.gov/news/releases/2004/12/20041217-15.html.

Bush Law: Real ID Act of 2005

Citation: Public Law 109-13.

Who is hurt by this law: This act requires everyone to have a national identity card by January 1, 2010, which will increase the risk of identity theft and enable the federal government to heighten its surveillance of innocent Americans.[1] (Terrorists are unlikely to be deterred and will simply create fraudulent documents.[2])

Because the act is an unfunded mandate, states and taxpayers will have to pay more than $11,000,000,000 to implement it at the onset and $10.5 billion more over the first five years.[3] State governments will have to remake their driver's licenses and overhaul their database systems in order to easily transfer individuals' records.[4] Alabama, which passed this law, sent 80,000 letters to people whose records were mismatched, warning them that their driver's licenses will be revoked. Alabama citizens rushed in large numbers to their local DMVs, panicked that they would lose their licenses.[5]

Seventeen states have passed resolutions declaring that they will not implement the Real ID program.[6]

What the law provides: The Real ID Act was included in a defense spending and tsunami relief bill. It provides that the federal government will take greater control over driver's license requirements, and federal agencies will not accept identification from states that do not comply (§202(a)). The Department of Homeland Security will require states to take digital images of all identity documents and store copies of them in a transferable format (§202(d)(1), (2), and (13)).

What the law ignores:

The privacy protections in the penumbra of the First and Ninth Amendments.

U.S. Constitution, Amend. 10: "The powers not delegated to the United States by the Constitution, nor prohibited by it to the States, are reserved to the States respectively, or to the people."

U.N. Charter, Arts. 55 and 56.

International Covenant on Civil and Political Rights (ICCPR), Art. 2(1).

ICCPR, Art. 17(1): "No one shall be subjected to arbitrary or unlawful interference with his privacy, family, or correspondence, nor to unlawful attacks on his honour and reputation."

ICERD, Art. 5(d)(i), (viii), (ix), and (e)(i), (iii-v).

Bills proposed to undo the Real ID Act:

S. 717: Identification Security Enhancement Act of 2007 (introduced 2/28/2007); sponsored by Sen. Daniel Akaka (D-HI) with 7 cosponsors.

H.R. 1117: REAL ID Repeal and Identification Security Enhancement Act of 2007 (introduced 2/16/2007); sponsored by Rep. Thomas Allen (D-ME) with 36 cosponsors.

What Congress can do: Congress can repeal the Real ID Act of 2005 or reintroduce and pass H.R. 1117 or S. 717.

See also: www.realnightmare.org

---

[1] http://www.realnightmare.org (6/17/08).

[2] http://www.realnightmare.org/about/1/ (6/17/08).

[3] http://www.realnightmare.org/images/File/Real_ID_Impact_Report_ FINAL_Sept19.pdf (6/17/08).

[4] http://www.realnightmare.org/about/1/ (6/17/08).

[5] Mark Harrison, License Confusion Possible, The Times-Journal, Oct. 1, 2005.

[6] http://washingtonindependent.com/view/is-real-id-really (6/18/08).

Bush "Law": Mismanagement of Hurricanes Katrina and Rita Relief Efforts

Who is hurt by this "law": The people in the Gulf Coast region who were hit by Hurricanes Katrina and Rita in August 2005 and did not get necessary assistance immediately after the storm and are still not getting the assistance they need now.

What the "law" provided: Immediately after Hurricane Katrina, Pres. Bush ordered the National Guard to "fight crime" rather than evacuate those stranded from lack of federal assistance. Nearly 150,000 people that lacked the means to evacuate the city suffered as a result.[1] In the U. N. Committee on the Elimination of Racial Discrimination's Concluding Observations, the Committee expressed concern for the "disparate impact that this natural disaster continues to have on low-income African American residents, many of whom continue to be displaced after more than two years after the hurricane" and recommended that the U.S. increase its efforts in returning displaced persons or provide adequate and affordable housing.[2]

30

In 2007, the Government Accountability Office (GAO) reported that the Federal Emergency Management Agency (FEMA) lost $30 million taxpayer dollars through "ineffective oversight" of housing contracts, which affects those still residing in FEMA trailers. FEMA paid $15 million for maintenance inspections, but has no record that those inspections took place; $600,000 for emergency repairs on trailers that do not exist in their inventory; and $4 million for a contract that only cost $800,000 when completed.[3] FEMA calculated it had $85 million surplus of dinnerware sets, towels, clothes, and cleaning items, so it gave them to federal agencies and sixteen states. Katrina and Rita victims desperately still need the FEMA supplies given away.[4]

What the "law" ignores:

U.S. Constitution, General Welfare Clause, Art. I, §8, cl. 1.
U.N. Charter, Preamble.
U.N. Charter, Art. 55 & 56.
ICCPR, Preamble.
ICCPR, Art. 2(1).
ICCPR, Art. 7.
ICCPR, Art. 9(1).
ICCPR, Art. 23(1).
ICAT, Art. 2(2).
ICAT, Art. 16(1).
ICERD, Art. 5.

Bills proposed to repeal the "law":

H.R. 3247: Hurricanes Katrina and Rita Recovery Facilitation Act of 2007 (introduced 7/30/07); sponsored by Del. Eleanor Norton (D-DC) with 6 cosponsors.

H.R. 265: Hurricane Katrina Disaster Inquiry Commission Act of 2007 (introduced 1/5/07); sponsored by Rep. Sheila Jackson-Lee (D-TX).

H.R. 1227: Gulf Coast Hurricane Housing Recovery Act of 2007 (passed House 3/21/07); sponsored by Rep. Maxine Waters (D-CA) with 1 cosponsor.

What Congress can do: In 2009, Congress members can: (1) reintroduce and pass the above bills; (2) pass new bills to bring the U.S. into compliance with CERD's Concluding Observations.
See also: GAO Report regarding Hurricane Katrina, http://www.gao.gov/new.items/d08106.pdf, (8/5/08).

[1] Malkia A. Cyril, *Racism or Relief, Alternet.org,* Sept. 8, 2005, http://www.alternet.org/katrina/25181/, (8/5/08).

[2] ICERD/C/USA/CO/6, 7/8/08.

[3] Government Accountability Office, *Report to the Committee on Homeland Security and Governmental Affairs, U.S. Senate,* Nov. 2007.

[4] Abbie Boudreau & Scott Zamost, *Supplies for Katrina Victims Went to Mississippi Agencies, CNN,* July 8, 2008.

Bush Law: Animal Enterprise Terrorism Act of 2006 (AETA)

Citation: Animal Enterprise Protection Act: Pub. L. 102-346; amended by Animal Enterprise Terrorism Act: 18 USC §43.

Who is hurt by this law: People peacefully demonstrating and leafleting at packing house companies/animal enterprises, conducting undercover investigations of such companies, and boycotting them. This provision might also apply to animal rights whistleblowers whose intentions are to stop harmful or illegal activities by the animal enterprise and serve as deterrence for whistleblowers. Anyone prosecuted under the Act will also be subject to the label, "terrorist," which causes reputational damage even if the accused prevails in court.

What the law provides: AETA broadly criminalizes First Amendment activities--from peaceful demonstrations to boycotts--although federal criminal laws already provided a wide range of punishments for unlawful activities targeting animal enterprises. AETA expands the class of criminal behavior in 18 U.S.C. §43, by changing the term used to describe activity "for the purpose of causing physical disruption" to activity "for the purpose of damaging or disrupting" an animal enterprise. The new Act also makes the expanded crime a predicate for Title III federal criminal wiretapping. A court will be far more likely to find probable cause for a vague crime of causing economic damage or disruption to an animal enterprise than for a crime that requires some evidence that the organization plans to engage in activity causing illegal "physical disruption."

What the law ignores:
U.S. Constitution, First Amendment.
U.N. Charter, Preamble.

International Covenant on Civil and Political Rights (ICCPR), Preamble.
ICCPR, Art. 19.

What Congress can do: The new Congress in 2009 can repeal the Animal Enterprise Terrorism Act.

See also: American Civil Liberties Union, http://www.aclu.org/freespeech/gen/2

Contributor: ACLU Washington Legislative Office

Bush "Law": Failure to Appoint Privacy and Civil Liberties Oversight Board

Citation: Implementing Recommendations of the 9/11 Commission Act of 2007 (IRCA) [H.R. 1- 2007]

Who is hurt by this "law": In its Final Report, the National Commission on Terrorist Attacks Upon the United States, (commonly referred to as The 9/11 Commission), declared: "we must find ways of reconciling security with liberty, since the success of one helps protect the other... Yet, if our liberties are curtailed, we lose the values that we are struggling to defend."[1] Should the provisions of the Implementing Recommendations of the 9/11 Commission Act of 2007 continue to be unexecuted, everyone in the U.S. risks the loss of our civil liberties.

What the "law" provides: In response to the 9/11 Commission's recommendation for a board within the Executive branch to oversee adherence to the guidelines the Commission recommended, and the commitment to defend civil liberties, the Intelligence Reform and Terrorism Prevention Act of 2004 (IRTPA) became law on Dec. 17, 2004 and established the Privacy and Civil Liberties Oversight Board, whose members were to be appointed by the President with approval of the Senate.[2] Privacy advocates and members of Congress decried both the President's appointees and their practices of "whitewash[ing]" the warrantless National Security Agency wiretapping program and allowing the White House to edit the reports of the Civil Liberties Board before they are issued.[3]

In response, Congress included Section 801 in IRCA of 2007, which terminated the tenure of the current board members and required the cooperation of the President and the Senate to appoint new members.[4] This newer bill also bestowed upon the Board the ability to issue subpoena requests, limit the oversight by the Attorney General, and required more frequent reports to Congress on their progress and findings.[5] In response Pres. Bush has made no appointments, the Board has no members, no offices, and all of its documents are being sent to the National Archives for storage.[6]

Sept. 20, 2008, U.S. District Judge Colleen Kollar-Kotelly issued a preliminary injunction in *Citizens for Responsibility and Ethics in Washington (CREW), et al. v. Cheney, et al.,* requiring Cheney, the Office of the Vice President, the Executive Office of the President, and the National Archives and Records Administration to preserve all vice presidential records relating to the vice president carrying out his constitutional, statutory or other official or ceremonial duties.[7]

What the "law" ignores:

U.S. Constitution, General Welfare Clause, Art. 1, Sec. 8, cl. 1.
U.S. Constitution, Art. II, Sec. 3.
U.S. Constitution, First Amendment.
U.S. Constitution, Fourth Amendment.
U.S. Constitution, Ninth Amendment.

What Congress can do: In 2009, Congress can insist that the new President immediately appoint members to the Privacy and Civil Liberties Oversight Board to ensure the recommendations of the 9/11 Commission are fully realized. Through the Implementing Recommendations of the 9/11 Commissions Act of 2007, Congress has created and empowered the new Board to protect the civil liberties from the encroachment of security needs.

In 2009 Congress can work with the new President to ensure he appoints members to the Board who will function in a non-partisan manner; perform their duties and not defer to the Executive Branch.

---

[1] Thomas Kean, et. al. "The 9/11 Commission Report." July 22, 2004. Retrieved on July 14, 2004 from <http://www.9-11commission.gov/report/911Report.pdf>.

[2] S. 2845--108th Congress (2004): Intelligence Reform and Terrorism Prevention Act of 2004. Sec. 1061.

[3] Ryan Singel. "Abracadabra! Bush Makes Privacy Board Vanish." Wired Magazine. Wired.com. February 4, 2008. Retrieved on July 14, 2008 from <http://www.wired.com/politics/onlinerights/news/2008/02/privacy_board>.

[4] H.R. 1--110th Congress (2007): Implementing Recommendations of the 9/11 Commission Act of 2007. Sec. 801. Retrieved on July 14, 2008 from <http://www.ise.gov/docs/nsis/Implementing911_Act.pdf>.

[5] Id.

[6] Supra, note 3.

[7] www.citizensforethics.org

See Also:

http://www.wired.com/politics/security/news/2004/08/64784
http://www.wired.com/politics/law/news/2004/08/64660
http://www.newsweek.com/id/145140/page/1
http://www.ise.gov/docs/nsis/Implementing911_Act.pdf
http://www.9-11commission.gov/report/911Report.pdf
http://www.newsweek.com/id/145847
http://www.wired.com/politics/onlinerights/news/2008/02/privacy_board

Bush Law: Foreign Intelligence Surveillance Act (FISA) Amendments Act of 2008

Citation: Public Law 110-261.

Who is hurt by this law: People in the U.S. and abroad are hurt by this law because it "essentially legalizes the president's unlawful warrantless wiretapping program..."[1] The FBI has been issuing National Security Letters (NSLs) to internet service providers, telecommunications companies, libraries, financial institutions, and credit card companies that require them to turn over information on their customers. There is also a gag order included in the NSLs that prohibit the companies from revealing that they received the NSL. The ACLU estimated that the FBI issued nearly 200,000 NSLs between 2003 and 2006.[2] Federal courts in 2007 struck down the NSL provision, but the federal government continues to appeal the decisions.[3] With the passage of the FISA Amendments Act, telecommunications companies will not be held liable for handing over information requested in the NSLs.

What the law provides: FISA was passed in 1978 and amended in 2001 by the USA PATRIOT Act. On July 10, 2008, Pres. Bush signed the FISA Amendments Act of 2008 that "grants absolute retroactive immunity to telecommunication companies that facilitated the president's warrantless wiretapping program over the last seven

35

years by ensuring the dismissal of court cases pending against those companies."[4]

The law only allows the Foreign Intelligence Surveillance Court (FISC) to review general procedure for spying, but not look at individual warrants. This permits the government to "conduct mass, untargeted surveillance of all communications coming into and out of the U.S., without any individualized review, and without any finding of wrongdoing."[5]

What the law ignores:
  U.S. Constitution, General Welfare Clause, Art. I, §8, cl. 1.
  U.S. Constitution, Fourth Amendment.
  U.S. Constitution, Fifth Amendment.
  The privacy protections in the penumbras of the First and Ninth Amendments.
  U.N. Charter, Preamble.
  U.N. Charter, Art. 55 & 56.
  International Covenant on Civil and Political Rights (ICCPR), Preamble.
  ICCPR, Art. 17(1): "No one shall be subjected to arbitrary or unlawful interference with his privacy, family, or correspondence, nor to unlawful attacks on his honour or reputation."

What Congress can do: In 2009, Congressmembers can repeal the FISA Amendments Act of 2008.

See also: American Civil Liberties Union, http://www.aclu.org/safefree/spying/

---

[1] ACLU, *Senate Passes Unconstitutional Spying Bill and Grants Sweeping Immunity to Phone Companies,* July 7, 2008.

[2] ACLU, *National Security Letters,* http://www.aclu.org/safefree/nationalsecurityletters/index.html, (8/4/08).

[3] *See: Doe v. Gonzales*, 500 F. Supp. 2d 379 (2007).

[4] ACLU, *Senate Passes Unconstitutional Spying Bill and Grants Sweeping Immunity to Phone Companies,* July 9, 2008.

[5] American Civil Liberties Union, *H.R. 6304, The FISA Amendments Act of 2008,* June 19, 2008, http://www.aclu.org/safefree/nsaspying/35731res20080619.html, (8/4/08).

Bush "Law": Violent Radicalization and Homegrown Terrorism Prevention Act of 2007

Citation: H.R. 1955 and S. 1959.

Who will be hurt by this "law": Any person in the U.S. who has a belief system that the government may consider "extremist" will be hurt by passage of this bill. "The definitions ...provided in S. 1959 are so broad that they could be used by the commission to investigate movements and activists in violation of their constitutional rights," according to the Center for Constitutional Rights.[1] This bill does not focus on criminal behavior but on ideology. It not only threatens free-speech, but reintroduces the concept of preventive detention based on beliefs rather than actions.[2] The bill specifically targets the internet, which has been upheld by the courts as a "free-speech zone" equal to that of books, newspapers, etc. This bill is one of many[3] put forward to increase surveillance and decrease civil liberties.

What the "law" provides:

Sec. 899C of the Act would cost around $22 million over four years to establish a national bipartisan commission to "[e]xamine and report upon the facts and causes of violent radicalization, homegrown terrorism, and ideologically based violence in the United States" through hearings and issuing reports. It would also amend the Homeland Security Act of 2002 (6 U.S.C. 361, et seq.) by including the following provisions:

§899A(2): "...The term 'violent radicalization' means the process of adopting or promoting an extremist belief system for the purpose of facilitating ideologically based violence to advance political, religious, or social change."

§899A(4): "...The term 'ideologically based violence' means the use, planned use, or threatened use of force or violence by a group or individual to promote the group or individual's political, religious, or social beliefs."

§899B(3): "The Internet has aided in facilitating violent radicalization, ideologically based violence, and the homegrown terrorism process in the United States by providing access to broad and constant streams of terrorist-related propaganda to the United States citizens."

What the "law" ignores:
U.S. Constitution, First Amendment.
U.S. Constitution, General Welfare Clause, Art. I. §8, cl. 2.
The right to privacy in the penumbra of the First and Ninth
    Amendments.
International Covenant on Civil and Political Rights
    (ICCPR), Art. 2(1).
ICCPR, Art. 9(1).
ICCPR, Art. 17(1).
ICCPR, Art. 18(1)
ICCPR, Art. 19: "(1) Everyone shall have the right to hold opinions
    without interference. (2) Everyone shall have the right to freedom
    of expression; this right shall include freedom to seek, receive and
    impart information and ideas of all kinds, regardless of frontiers,
    either orally, in writing or in print, in the form of art, or through
    any media of his choice.

What Congress can do: In 2009, Congressmembers can not
reintroduce this bill.

---

[1] Center for Constitutional Rights, Here Come the Thought Police: *The
Violent Radicalization and Homegrown Terrorism Prevention Act of
2007*, http://ccrjustice.org/learn-more/faqs/factsheet%3A-violent-
radicalization-and-homegrown-terrorism-prevention-act-2007, (7/15/08).
[2] Id.
[3] *See also* FISA and the USA PATRIOT ACT

DETENTION/HABEAS CORPUS

Bush Law: Habeas Corpus as to Detainees Suspended

See also: Military Commissons Act, *infra*

Citation: Military Commissions Act of 2006 (MCA)(Pub. L. No. 109-336, 120 Stat. 2616): Sec. 7(a) and Authorization for Use of Military Force (Pub. L. No. 107-40, § 2(a), Sept. 18, 2001).

Who is hurt by this law: The U.S. has arrested at least 775 individuals worldwide as "enemy combatants"[1] and held them in indefinite detention at Guantanamo Bay in Cuba, Abu Ghraib in Iraq, and elsewhere. Of these detainees, at least 40 attempted suicide,[2] three succeeded in committing suicide.[3] At least 128 other men went on hunger strikes until U.S. soldiers force fed them. The U.S. still holds 270 detainees at Guantanamo Bay Naval Base in Cuba.[4]

What the law provides: "...No court, justice, or judge shall have jurisdiction to hear or consider an application for a writ of habeas corpus filed by or on behalf of an alien detained by the United States who has been determined by the United States to have been properly detained as an enemy combatant or is awaiting such determination."

39

This Bush law ignores:

U.S. Constitution Art. I, Sec. 2, Cl. 2: "The Privilege of the Writ of Habeas Corpus shall not be suspended, unless when in Cases of Rebellion or Invasion the public Safety may require it."

U.N. Charter, Art. 55: "The United Nations [and member nations] shall promote:...(c) universal respect for, and observance of, human rights and fundamental freedoms for all without distinction as to race, sex, language, or religion."

ICCPR, Art. 9(1): "Everyone has the right to liberty and security of person. No one shall be subjected to arbitrary arrest or detention. No one shall be deprived of his liberty except on such grounds and in accordance with such procedure as are established by law."

ICCPR, Art. 9(2): "Anyone who is arrested shall be informed, at the time of arrest, of the reasons for his arrest and shall be promptly informed of any charges against him."

ICERD, Art. 5: "...Parties undertake...to guarantee the right of everyone, without distinction as to race, colour, or national or ethnic origin, to equality before the law, notably in the enjoyment of the following rights: (a) The right to equal treatment before the tribunals an all other organs administering justice;"

Bills introduced in 2007 restoring habeas corpus:

S.185: Habeas Corpus Restoration Act of 2007, sponsored by Sen. Arlen Specter (R-PA) with 31 cosponsors

H.R.1416: Habeas Corpus Restoration Act of 2007, sponsored by Rep. Jerrold Nadler (D-NY) with 86 cosponsors

What Congress can do: In 2009, Congressmembers can immediately introduce and pass bills repealing the MCA or reintroduce the bills that would restore habeas corpus to detainees.

See also: http://www.aclu.org/safefree/detention/ commissions.html

---

[1] www.defenselink.mil, *News Releases*, Dec. 20, 2007, (5/27/08).

[2] Carol J. Williams, *LA Times,* May 19, 2006.

[3] Carol D. Leonnig, *Washington Post,* Sept. 13, 2005.

[4] www.defenselink.mil, *News Releases*, May 2, 2008, (5/7/08).

Bush "Law": 2002 and 2003 Torture Memos by John Yoo and Jay Bybee

Citation: Memorandum Re: Application of Treaties and Laws to al Qaeda and Taliban Detainees, Jan. 9, 2002.

Who is hurt by this "law": Anyone who was or is interrogated and/or tortured by the U.S. military or the CIA is hurt by these Memos because their goal is to justify the detention and interrogation of detainees, and allow the Executive branch to avoid liability for these actions. Jay Bybee and John Yoo of the Office of Legal Counsel (OLC) wrote these Memos in 2002 and 2003.

Specifically, those detainees subjected to waterboarding are also harmed because the Department of Justice has avoided classifying waterboarding as "torture." Whether courts will rule that waterboarding is "torture" or won't, the practice violates the prohibition against inflicting cruel and unusual punishment.[1] But those people who have been subjected to it or will be subjected to it in the future are left without any meaningful recourse for compensation. This interrogation practice is a technique used during the Spanish Inquisition to coerce confessions and involves putting a cloth, sack, or plastic bag over the victim's mouth and then pouring water into his mouth to simulate drowning.[2] It is used because "it causes great physical and mental suffering, yet leaves no marks on the body."[3] There have been numerous debates in the media and hearings in Congress on whether waterboarding qualifies as torture. Attorney General Michael Mukasey, during his confirmation hearing, stated, "if it amounts to torture, it is not constitutional," but avoided the issue further by refusing to say whether it qualifies as "torture." [4]

What the "law" provides: The 2002 Memos offer legal justification for why U.S. officials are not liable for war crimes for the torture and interrogation techniques used on detainees. These Memos advised that the Executive branch does not have to comply with the Geneva Conventions[5] and the War Crimes Act of 1996[6] because they claim neither applies to al Qaeda or the Taliban.[7] Shortly after the release of the first Memo, Alberto Gonzales, as White House Counsel, advised Pres. Bush to declare that members of al Qaeda and the Taliban are beyond the reach of the Geneva Conventions.[8] The OLC claimed this declaration absolved those who were previously at risk of being charged with war crimes.

Another Memo, in 2003, declared that Pres. Bush was not bound by international treaty law that prohibited torture or by the Anti-Torture Act.[9] This Memo justified the claim by citing Commander-in-Chief authority to protect the nation. The Executive branch has cited national security and the Commander-in-Chief power as a justification for a wide range of activities, including everything from warrantless wiretapping to indefinite detention to torture.

What the "law" ignores:

U.S. Constitution, Art. I, §9, cl. 2. Habeas Corpus.
U.S. Constitution, Fifth Amendment.
U.S. Constitution, Eighth Amendment: cruel and unusual punishment.
War Crimes Act of 1996, 18 U.S.C. Part I, Ch. 118, §2441.
Anti-Torture Statute, 18 U.S.C. Part I, Ch. 113C, §2340(1).
U.N. Charter, Preamble.
U.N. Charter, Art. 55 & 56.
Geneva Convention re Treatment of Prisoners of War, Art. 118.
ICCPR, Preamble.
ICCPR, Art. 2(1).
ICCPR, Art. 7.
ICCPR, Art. 10(1).
ICAT, Art. 2(1)(2).
ICAT, Art. 5(1)(2).
ICAT, Art. 11.
ICAT, Art. 16(1).

Bills proposed to repeal the "law":

S. 1876: National Security with Justice Act (introduced 7/25/07); sponsored by Sen. Joseph Biden (D-DE) with 2 cosponsors.

H.R. 5460: To amend the Detainee Treatment Act of 2005 and 18 U.S. Code, to include waterboarding in the definition of cruel, inhuman, or degrading treatment or punishment and in the definition of torture, (introduced 2/14/08); sponsored by Rep. Anna Eshoo (D-CA) with 1 cosponsor.

S. 1943: To establish uniform standards for interrogation techniques applicable to individuals under the custody or physical control of the U.S. Government (introduced 8/2/07); sponsored by Sen. Edward Kennedy (D-MA) with 7 cosponsors.

H.R. 4114: American Anti-Torture Act of 2007 (introduced 11/8/07); sponsored by Rep. Jerrold Nadler (D-NY) with 79 cosponsors.

H.R. 5167: Justice for Victims of Torture and Terrorism Act (introduced 1/29/08); sponsored by Rep. Bruce Braley (D-IA) with 35 cosponsors.

H.R. 3541: PRISE Act of 2005 (introduced 7/28/05); sponsored by Rep. John Conyers (D-MI) with 6 cosponsors.

What Congress can do: In 2009, Congressmembers can:
Reintroduce and pass the above bills;
Pass a resolution declaring that waterboarding is torture;
Amend the War Crimes Act of 1996 and the Anti-Torture Statute to specifically include "waterboarding" in the definition of "torture."
See also: "Law of Torture & Holding Accountable Those Who Are Complicit in Approving Torture of Persons in U.S. Custody," National Lawyers Guild & International Association of Democratic Lawyers: www.nlg.org/news/statements/NLGWhitePaper_Yoo.doc

---

[1] See also "What the 'law' ignores" below.

[2] Eric Weiner, *Waterboarding: A Tortured History, NPR,* Nov. 3, 2007.

[3] Id.

[4] Senate Judiciary Committee Hearing for Nomination of Judge Mukasey as Attorney General, Day Two. October 18, 2007 http://www.washingtonpost.com/wp-srv/politics/documents/transcript_mukasey_hearing_day_two_101807.html

[5] Geneva Convention re Treatment of Prisoners of War, Art. 118, Aug. 12, 1949, 6 U.S.T. 3316.

[6] 18 U.S.C. Part I, Ch. 118, §2441.

[7] John Yoo to William J. Haynes, Memorandum Re: Application of Treaties and Laws to al Qaeda and Taliban Detainees, Jan. 9, 2002.

[8] Neil A. Lewis, *A Guide to the Memos on Torture, New York Times,* http://www.nytimes.com/ref/international/24MEMO-GUIDE.html, (7/30/08).

[9] Id.

Bush "Law": Black Sites and Extraordinary Rendition

Citation: Presidential Directive on Sept. 17, 2001 by Pres. George W. Bush building on Pres. Directive 39 on June 21, 1995 by Pres. William J. Clinton.

Who is hurt by this "law": At least 100 individuals are known to have been captured and detained in the Central Intelligence Agency's (CIA) covert prison system locations, "black sites," and many more may be in prisons not yet discovered. The U.S. has also been engaging in extraordinary rendition, when the CIA hands over terrorist suspects to other countries who do not have U. S. anti-torture laws. The CIA forcibly apprehends those it suspects have terrorist connections and transports them to "black sites" because these locations are outside the legal jurisdiction and mainland U.S. territory and function as a covert prison system with very little public oversight. Only the President and a few senior officials actually know the locations and scope of the black sites. In Congress, only the chair and vice chair of the House and Senate Intelligence Committees know the generalities of the program. Some of the countries where the CIA has established black sites, either in the past or at present, are Thailand, Morocco, Pakistan, Syria, Afghanistan, Egypt, Saudi Arabia, and Qatar. During their detention, suspects are not permitted to contact a lawyer or their families, nor are they charged with any crime or allowed to meet with International Committee of the Red Cross (ICRC).[1]

During detention, the CIA uses "enhanced interrogation techniques" including exposure to loud music for prolonged periods, exposure to cold temperatures without clothes, never turning the lights off, and isolation for months or years.[2] Even if some of the detainees claim that they were not physically beaten, being kidnapped and held in isolation for months or years at a time combined with the conditions of the prisons leads to "extreme psychological anguish."[3]

What the "law" provides: Pres. Clinton issued Presidential Directive 39: "if we do not receive adequate cooperation from a state that harbors a terrorist whose extradition we are seeking, we shall take appropriate measures to induce cooperation. Return of suspects by force may be effective without the cooperation of the host government...." This established extraordinary rendition and the Bush Administration greatly expanded the program after 9/11. On Sept. 17, 2001, Pres. Bush signed a directive to give the CIA broad authority to kill, capture, and detain terrorists including al Qaeda members.[4] This directive remains classified. In a letter to the ACLU, the Department of Justice acknowledged its existence[5] and Pres. Bush has publicly acknowledged the existence of the black sites.[6]

What the "law" ignores:

U.S. Constitution, Art. I, §9, cl. 2.
U.S. Constitution, Fifth Amendment.
U.S. Constitution, Eighth Amendment.
War Crimes Act of 1996, 18 U.S.C. Part I, Ch. 118, §2441.
Anti-Torture Statute, 18 U.S.C. Part I, Ch. 113C, §2340(1).
U.N. Charter, Preamble.
U.N. Charter, Art. 55 & 56.
Geneva Convention Relative to the Treatment of Prisoners of
  War, Art. 118.
ICCPR, Preamble.
ICCPR, Art. 2(1).
ICCPR, Art. 7.
ICCPR, Art. 9(1)(2)(3)(4).
ICCPR, Art. 10(1).
ICCPR, Art. 14(3).
ICCPR, Art. 16(1).
ICCPR, Art. 23(1).
ICAT, Art. 2(1)(2).
ICAT, Art. 3(1)(2).
ICAT, Art. 5(1)(2).
ICAT, Art. 11.
ICAT, Art. 16(1).

Bills proposed to undo the "law":

S. 1876: National Security with Justice Act (introduced 7/25/
  07); sponsored by Sen. Joseph Biden (D-DE) with 2 cosponsors.

S. 1943: A bill to establish uniform standards for interrogation
  techniques applicable to individuals under the custody or
  physical control of the U. S. Government (introduced 8/2/07);
  sponsored by Sen. Edward Kennedy (D-MA) with 7 cosponsors.

H.R. 1352: Torture Outsourcing Prevention Act (introduced
  3/6/07); sponsored by Rep. Edward Markey (D-MA) with 60
  cosponsors.

H.R. 4114: American Anti-Torture Act of 2007 (introduced
  11/8/07); sponsored by Rep. Jerrold Nadler (D-NY) with 79
  cosponsors.

H.R. 5167: Justice for Victims of Torture and Terrorism Act
  (introduced 1/29/08); sponsored by Rep. Bruce Braley (D-IA)
  with 35 cosponsors.

S. 654: Convention Against Torture Implementation Act of 2005 (introduced 3/17/05); sponsored by Sen. Patrick Leahy (D-VT) with 8 cosponsors.

H.R. 3541: PRISE Act of 2005 (introduced 7/28/05); sponsored by Rep. John Conyers (D-MI) with 6 cosponsors.

H.Con.Res. 101: Calling on the President to order an immediate moratorium on the rendition of persons to Syria and all countries that routinely use torture as reported by the Department of State's 2004 Country Reports on Human Rights Practices, and for other purposes (introduced 3/16/05); sponsored by Rep. Betty McCollum (D-MN) with 1 cosponsor.

What Congress can do: In 2009, Congressmembers can reintroduce and pass the above bills.

See also: PBS, World Extraordinary Rendition: Mapping the Black Sites: http://www.pbs.org/frontlineworld/stories/rendition701/map/, (7/29/08).

---

[1] Dana Priest, *CIA Holds Terrorism Suspects in Secret Prisons, Washington Post,* Nov. 2, 2002.

[2] Mark Benjamin, *Inside the CIA's Notorious "Black Sites," Salon.com,* Dec. 14, 2007, http://www.salon.com/news/feature/2007/12/14/bashmilah/index.html, (7/28/08).

[3] Id.

[4] Dana Priest, *CIA Holds Terrorism Suspects in Secret Prisons, Washington Post,* Nov. 2, 2002.

[5] Letter from Peter Skinner of United States Attorney's Office, Southern District of New York, to Lawrence S. Lustberg, Melanca D. Clark, and Amrit Singh, November 9, 2006, http://www.aclu.org/images/torture/asset_upload_file825_27365.pdf, (7/28/08).

[6] White House, Office of the Press Secretary, "President Discusses Creation of Military Commissions to Try Suspected Terrorists," Sept. 6, 2006

Bush Policy: No Enforceable Department of Homeland Security (DHS) Regulations to Protect Immigration Detainees

Citation: DHS Detention Operations Manual (2006).

Who is hurt by the lack of enforceable regulations: In 2007, DHS detained approximately 300,000 immigrants, primarily based on charges of non-criminal immigration violations. On any given day, DHS holds approximately 30,000 immigrants in custody in locations all across the U.S. pending administrative deportation proceedings. Detainees do not have a trial, a judge and jury, proof beyond a reasonable doubt, or a court appointed attorney.[1] Few of the due process protections in the Administrative Procedure Act (APA) apply.

"DHS is one of the largest jailers in the world," said Paromita Shah, Associate Director of the National Immigration Project of the National Lawyers Guild, one of the plaintiffs in a lawsuit against Michael Chertoff, Secretary of DHS, seeking comprehensive and enforceable regulations governing detention standards for immigration detainees. "But it behaves like a lawless local sheriff. The refusal to adopt comprehensive, binding regulations has contributed to a system in which thousands of immigration detainees are routinely denied necessary medical care, visitation, legal materials, or functioning telephones." Rafiu Abimola says "I was detained for six years...[t]he telephones frequently did not work and legal materials were unavailable or out of date. Because I was managing my case on my own, this was extremely hard for me. DHS did not attempt to fix these problems. When I complained to the jail, I never received a response, and sometimes was punished for complaining. There are no consequences to the government for failing to obey its own standards."[2]

What the current "law" provides: No federally-mandated regulations exist, resulting in inconsistent and substandard living conditions, grossly inadequate medical care, and widespread abuse of detainee rights. Recent government reports have documented extensive patterns of non-compliance with the Detention Operations Manual. In addition to using its own facilities, DHS contracts with city, county, and state jails and privately operated prisons for this purpose.

47

What the lack of regulations ignores:

U.S. Constitution, General Welfare Clause, Art. 1, §8, cl. 2.
U.S. Constitution, Fifth Amendment, Due Process Clause.
U.N. Charter, Preamble.
U.N. Charter, Art. 55 & 56.
International Covenant on Civil and Political Rights
   (ICCPR), Preamble.
ICCPR, Art. 2(1).
ICCPR, Art. 7.
ICCPR, Art. 10(1).
ICCPR, Art. 10(3).
ICAT, Art. 11.
ICAT, Art. 16(1).
ICERD, Art. 2(1) (2).
ICERD, Art. 5.

Bills proposed to fix the lack of enforceable regulations:

H.R. 5950: Detainee Basic Medical Care Act of 2008
   (introduced 5/1/08); sponsored by Rep. Zoe Lofgren (D-CA)
   with 15 cosponsors.

S. 3005: Detainee Basic Medical Care Act of 2008 (introduced
   5/12/08); sponsored by Sen. Robert Menendez (D-NJ) with 6
   cosponsors.

S. 3114: Secure and Safe Detention and Asylum Act (introduced
   6/11/08); sponsored by Sen. Joseph Lieberman (I-CT) with 3
   cosponsors.

What Congress can do: In 2009, Congressmembers can:

Pass the above bills in relation to detainees' health care
   (*See also:* Inadequate Health Care in Immigration Detention
   Facilities, below)
Promulgate enforceable regulations.
Provide funding for the enforcement of federally-mandated
   regulations.
Encourage DHS to settle the lawsuit.
Hold hearings on how to ensure that due process is provided to
   immigration detainees.
Provide federal funding for federal detention facilities to
   decrease the ad hoc nature of local detention facilities.
Amend the Administrative Procedure Act to cover immigration
   agencies.

See also: http://www.detentionwatchnetwork.org

Contributor: Dan Kesselbrenner, National Immigration Project, National Lawyers Guild.

---
[1] *Bilokumsky v. Tod*, 263 U. S. 149 (1923).

[2] *National Immigration Project of the National Lawyers Guild, Families for freedom, Rafiu Abimola, et al v. Michale Chertoff, Secretary, Department of Hopmeland Security* (SD NY).

Bush Policy: Inadequate Healthcare in Immigration Detention Facilities

Who is hurt by the lack of healthcare: The 300,000 men, women, and children that are detained at over 400 detention facilities across the U.S. each year are at risk of death and injuries while detained because of inadequate healthcare at these facilities.[1] "Over 83 detainees have died in, or soon after, custody during the past five years," charges a *Washington Post* report.[2] Fifteen of the 83 deaths have been suicides because of the lack of mental healthcare for the 4,500 detainees that are mentally ill.[3] Their investigation also found that immigrants awaiting deportation suffered because of "flawed medical judgments, faulty administrative practices, neglectful guards, ill-trained technicians, sloppy-record keeping, lost medical files, and dangerous staff shortages."[4] Infectious diseases--tuberculosis and chicken pox--are spreading inside these facilities. Immigration and Customs Enforcement (ICE) has been detaining an increasing number of immigrants, which results in over-crowding and unsafe conditions at these facilities.[5] The population has nearly tripled, but spending on medical care for these facilities has not even doubled, according to ICE statistics. The U.S. government, via the U.S. Public Health Service, is responsible for detainee medical care, but many of the facilities use privately contracted medical staff.[6]

What the Bush Policy provides: Before their deportation hearing, a person is placed in civil immigration detention, because immigration law violations are not considered criminal charges. Detainees are not entitled to the protections prisoners get, such as the right to an attorney. ICE has agreements with numerous jails and prisons across the country to hold detainees until they have their hearing.

What ICE ignores:

U.S. Constitution, General Welfare Clause, Art. 1, §8, cl. 2.
U.N. Charter, Preamble.
U.N. Charter, Art. 55 & 56.
ICCPR, Preamble.
ICCPR, Art. 7.
ICCPR, Art. 10(1).
ICCPR, Art. 23(1).
ICAT, Art. 10(1).
ICAT, Art. 16(1).
ICERD, Art. 2(1).
ICERD, Art 2(2).
ICERD, Art. 5.

Bills proposed to improve the lack of healthcare:

H.R. 5950/S. 3005 Detainee Basic Medical Care Act of 2008
(introduced 5/1/08); sponsored by Rep. Zoe Lofgren (D-CA)
with 15 cosponsors and (introduced 5/12/08); sponsored by
Sen. Robert Menendez (D-NJ) with 6 cosponsors.

S. 3114: Secure and Safe Detention and Asylum Act (introduced
6/11/08); sponsored by Sen. Joseph Lieberman (I-CT) with 3
cosponsors.

What Congress can do: In 2009, Congressmembers can:

Discontinue funding ICE until it allocates and safeguards enough
money to cover all medical care for detainees.

Pass the Detainee Basic Medical Care Act (H.R. 5950/S. 3005),
which requires the Dept. of Homeland Security to develop
procedures for providing adequate health care to immigrants
held in ICE detention.

Discontinue funding ICE until it promulgates regulations for
the treatment of immigrants in detention that incorporate
recommendations filed by NGOs and detained immigrants in
the 2007 petition for rulemaking.

See also: http://www.detentionwatchnetwork.org

Contributor: Dan Kesselbrenner, National Immigration Project of
the National Lawyers Guild.

---

[1] Dana Priest and Amy Goldstein, *System of Neglect: Part 1, Washington
Post*, May 11, 2008.

[2] Id.

[3] Dana Priest and Amy Goldstein, *System of Neglect: Part 3, Washington Post,* May 13, 2008.

[4] Dana Priest and Amy Goldstein, *System of Neglect: Part 1, Washington Post,* May 11, 2008.

[5] Id.

[6] Id.

Bush "Law": Statement on Signing the Department of Defense Emergency Supplemental Appropriations to Address Hurricanes in the Gulf of Mexico, and Pandemic Influenza Act of 2006.

Citation: 41 Weekly Comp. Pres. Doc. 1918 (Dec. 30, 2005).

Who is hurt by this "law": Everyone subjected to interrogation by U.S. officials since the beginning of 2006 has been hurt by this Bush signing statement negating the protections against cruel and degrading treatment, including everyone affected by the hurricanes in the Gulf of Mexico or in any way infected with the Bird Flu/pandemic influenza.

What the "law" provides: The President signed the Emergency Supplemental Appropriations Act to address two major health dangers but issued a signing statement directing the executive branch to interpret the law as preserving his authority to direct any sort of treatment of detainees, and that his decisions and executive actions were not subject to judicial review.

What the "law" ignores:
U.S. Constitution, Art. I, §7, cl. 2: on signing/vetoing.
U.S. Constitution, Eighth Amendment.
U.S. Constitution, Separation of Powers in Art. I, II, and III.
U.N. Charter, Preamble.
U.N. Charter, Arts. 55 & 56.
ICCPR, Art. 7.
ICCPR, Art. 9(1).
ICAT, Art. 2, 2(2).
ICAT, Art. 10(1).
ICERD, Art. 2(1).
ICERD, Art. 5.

What Congress can do: In 2009, Congress can: (1) pass Sen. Arlen Specter's (R-PA) Presidential Signing Statements Act, S. 3731, 109th Cong. instructing the federal courts to disregard signing statements and provide standing to Congressmembers who wish to challenge such statements in court; (2) pass legislation clarifying that signing statements, including this one, do not alter the requirements of the law; (3) refuse to confirm any nominees for office until they make clear that they understands that their duty is to the law as passed by Congress and signed by the President, without regard to signing statements or other anti-democratic maneuvers.

Contributor: Professor Zachary Wolfe, George Washington University

EDUCATION

No Child Left Behind Act of 2001 (NCLB)
Student and Exchange Visitor Information System (SEVIS)

Bush Law: No Child Left Behind Act of 2001 (NCLB)

Citation: Pub. L. 107-110, 20 U.S.C. §6301, Jan. 8, 2002.

Who is hurt by this law: The NCLB is an "unfunded mandate" requiring schools to meet NCLB standards.[1] States are spending millions of their own education budgets to meet its standards,[2] which force teachers to teach the answers to the test questions on mathematics and reading, rather than teaching science, social studies, and art.[3] Teacher Mark Lichtenberg: "NCLB's primary focus on math and reading has led to arts programs nationwide becoming less and less important or being completely removed from the curriculum."[4] By 2008, over 160 students in six classrooms in a South Bronx middle school refused to take yet another standardized NCLB test.[5] The act provides that test scores of minority and disadvantaged students do not count when their numbers are small, so schools have no incentive to provide these students with the same education as their fellow students.[6]

What the law provides: To receive federal funding for education, states must subject their students to numerous standardized tests used in "academic assessments" (Part A, §1111(b)(3)) to show that they are making "adequate yearly progress" (Part A, §1111(b)(2)(B)(C)).

What the law ignores:
U.S. Constitution, General Welfare Clause, Art. I, §8, cl. 1.
U.N. Charter, Art. 55.
ICCPR, Art. 2(1).

54

ICCPR, Art. 24(1).

ICAT, Art. 16.

ICERD, Preamble.

ICERD, Art. 2, §1(a).

Convention on the Rights of the Child (CRC), Art. 2(1).[7]

CRC, Art. 3(1).

CRC, Art. 13(1): "The child shall have the right to freedom of expression; this right shall include freedom to seek, receive and impart information and ideas of all kinds, regardless of frontiers, either orally, in writing or in print, in the form of art, or through any other media of the child's choice.

CRC, Art. 28(1): "States Parties recognize the right of the child to education, and with a view to achieving this right progressively and on the basis of equal opportunity, they shall, in particular: (a) Make primary education compulsory and available free to all; (b) Encourage the development of different forms of secondary education, including general and vocational education, make them available and accessible to every child, and take appropriate measures such as the introduction of free education and offering financial assistance in case of need; (c) Make higher education accessible to all on the basis of capacity by every appropriate means; (d) Make educational and vocational information and guidance available and accessible to all children; (e) Take measures to encourage regular attendance at schools and the reduction of drop-out rates."

Bills proposed to amend NCLB: Congressmembers have proposed over 31 bills amending the NCLB, none of which has passed.

What Congress can do: Repeal the No Child Left Behind Act or pass several of the bills to amend the Act:

S.1194 and H.R. 2087: No Child Left Behind Reform Act: Allows schools to be given credit for performing well on measures other than test scores when calculating student achievement. (introduced 4/24/07); sponsored by Sen. Christopher Dodd (D-CT) with 3 cosponsors (introduced 5/1/08); sponsored by Rep. Rosa DeLauro (D-CT) with 28 cosponsors;

S.1981: No Child Left Inside Act of 2007: Authorizes the use of funds under the Fund for the Improvement of Education program to advance environmental education. (introduced

7/12/07); sponsored by Sen. John Reed (D-RI) with 14 cosponsors;

H.R.3036: No Child Left Inside Act of 2007: Amends the Elementary and Secondary Education Act of 1965 to authorize states to use federal funds for the development of kindergarten through grade 12 (K-12) plans for environmental education and teacher training to ensure that high school graduates are environmentally literate. (introduced 7/12/07); sponsored by Rep. John Sarbanes (D-MD) with 64 cosponsors;

S.1775: No Child Left Behind Act of 2007: Establishes: (1) the Striving Readers grant program; (2) the Math Now grant program; (3) the Teacher Incentive Fund program; (4) the Adjunct Teachers Corps; (5) mentoring grant programs under the 21st Century Community Learning Centers program; (6) the Education Flexibility Partnership program; and (7) the Child-Centered program. (introduced 7/12/07); sponsored by Sen. Richard Burr (R-NC) with 3 cosponsors.

---

[1] http://www.nea.org/lawsuit/nr050420.html (6/2/08).

[2] http://www.nea.org/lawsuit/absurdities.html (6/2/08).

[3] Center on Education Policy, Choices, Changes, and Challenges: Curriculum and Instruction in the NCLB Era.

[4] http://www.nea.org/esea/nclbstories/nclbin07.html (6/3/08).

[5] Juan Gonzalez, *NY Daily News,* May 21, 2008.

[6] Jamie McKenzie, *NoChildLeft.com.*(6/3/08).

[7] The U.S. signed the Convention in 1995, but has yet to ratify it. The U.S. and Somalia are the only countries in the world that have not ratified the CRC. *The relevant text is featured in the Appendix.*

Bush "Law": Student and Exchange Visitor Information System (SEVIS)

Citation: Illegal Immigration Reform and Immigrant Responsibility Act (IIRAIRA): Public Law 104-208, Div. C, 110 Stat. 3009-546 and the USA PATRIOT Act: Public Law 107-56, 115 Stat. 272.

Who is hurt by this "law": There are one million foreign and international students and their dependents[1] that are hurt by this information monitoring and tracking database. According to commentators, SEVIS creates a mechanism to unfairly single out students based on their race or nationality. [2] They also say it violates student privacy because their personal information is available to numerous government agencies and students are the ones that must pay the costs for this program. SEVIS keeps track of information about a student's arrival, departure, school transfer, marriage status, dependents, country of origin, and other personal information.[3] Critics claim SEVIS is yet another example of increased government surveillance and intrusions on personal privacy that the Bush Administration has instituted.[4]

What the "law" provides: The IIRAIRA was passed in 1996, but in response to 9/11, Pres. Bush implemented the provision of this act that called for a surveillance mechanism for foreign students. SEVIS is a computer database that is used to track and monitor schools and international students while they are in the United States. Immigrations and Customs Enforcement (ICE), an executive agency under the umbrella of the Department of Homeland Security (DHS), is responsible for overseeing the database and providing students' information to other executive government departments and agencies, such as the Department of State, the Department of Energy, the Federal Bureau of Investigation (FBI), and the Central Intelligence Agency (CIA).

What the "law" ignores:

U.S. Constitution, General Welfare Clause, Art. I, §8, cl. 1.
The privacy protections in the penumbra of the First and Ninth Amendments.
U.N. Charter, Art. 55 & 56.
ICCPR, Preamble.
ICCPR, Art. 17(1).
ICERD, Art. 5.

What Congress can do: In 2009, Congressmembers can introduce legislation aimed at repealing the portions of the IIRAIRA and the USA PATRIOT Act that create and implement this monitoring program.

See also: Electronic Privacy Information Center, http://epic.org/privacy/surveillance/spotlight/0905/

---

[1] U.S. Immigration and Customs Enforcement, *Frequently Asked Questions: Student Exchange Visitor Program,* April 11, 2008, http://www.ice.gov/doclib/sevis/pdf/sevpfaq.pdf, (8/8/08).
[2] Refuse and Resist: Hawai'i Chapter, *Campaign to Stop SEVIS,* http:

//www.refuseandresist.org/newresistance/072402stopsevis.html, (8/8/08).

[3] Id.

[4] *See also*: USA PATRIOT Act, REAL ID Act, FISA Amendments Act, Animal Enterprise Terrorism Act, Homeland Security Act, Violent Radicalization and Homegrown Terrorism Act.

ELECTIONS

Bush Law: Help America Vote Act of 2002

Citation: Public Law 107-252.

Who is hurt by this Bush Law:

Every U.S. voter who is forced to vote using machines that are overly complicated in their presentation of the ballot, that have histories of misreporting votes, and that do not leave a paper trail should a recount or auditing need to be conducted.[1] Paper trails are vital to vesting in elections a form of legitimacy and certainty that reliance solely on electronic records cannot provide. Methods to reduce the potential for voter fraud have in effect proved to be restrictive of voter access to their ballots.[2]

Restrictive photo ID requirements and complicated voter registration processes also hurt potential voters.[3]

What the Law provides: The law promotes electronic voting machines over traditional punch-card machines that cause a new set of problems. The act does not require that a paper trail be left. HAVA also provides for the creation of the Election Assistance Commission, "an independent entity" charged with "serv[ing] as a national clearinghouse and resource for the compilation of information and review of procedures with respect to the administration of Federal elections."[4] Under Pres. Bush, the media has reported that this organization has been politicized to a degree rendering it incapable of carrying out those duties in an impartial manner beneficial to the electoral process.[5]

An application for voter registration for an election for Federal office may not be accepted or processed by a State unless the application includes-- (i) in the case of an applicant who has been issued a current and valid driver's license, the applicant's driver's license number; or (ii) in the case of any other applicant (other than an applicant to whom clause (ii) applies), the last 4 digits of the applicant's social security number."

Sec. 303 (b)(2): "Requirements.-- (A) In general.--An individual meets the requirements of this paragraph if the individual-- (i) in the case of an individual who votes in person-- (I) presents to the appropriate State or local election official a current and valid photo identification; or (II) presents to the appropriate State or local election official a copy of a current utility bill, bank statement, government check, paycheck, or other government document that shows the name and address of the voter..."

Help Americans Vote Act of 2002 ignores:

U.S. Constitution, Art. 1, General Welfare Clause, Sec. 8, cl. 1.

U.S. Constitution, 14th Amendment, cl. 1.

ICCPR, Art. 25(a, b).

What Congress can do: In 2009, Congress can support such members as Rep. Rush Holt (D-NJ) in their attempts to add to HAVA an amendment requiring that states produce paper trails in their election procedure and HAVA to allow each state to determine its own voting methods providing they guarantee to voters that their votes have been properly recorded and that such methods leave a viable paper trail so that contentions of voter fraud and corporate interference are made obsolete.

Congress can ensure that the EAC maintain a non-partisan atmosphere to facilitate the realization of the EAC's goals and objectives.

---

[1] Miles Rapoport. "Beyond Voting Machines: HAVA and Real Election Reform." Alternet.org. July 30, 2003. Retrieved on July 1, 2008 from <http://www.alternet.org/story/16490/>.

[2] "Restrictive Voter Identification Requirements." ProjectVote.org. Retrieved on July 1, 2008 from <http://projectvote.org/fileadmin/ ProjectVote/Policy_Briefs/Project_Vote_Policy_Brief_8_Voter_ ID.pdf>.

[3] *Id.*

[4] Help America Vote Act of 2002, Public Law 107-252 Sec. 201-202

[5] Tova Andrea Wang. "A Rigged Report on U.S. Voting?" WashingtonPost.com. August 30, 2007. Retrieved on July 1, 2008 from <http://www.washingtonpost.com/wp-dyn/content/article/2007/08/ 29/AR2007082901928.html?hpid=opinionsbox1.>.

ENERGY/ECOLOGY/ENVIRONMENT

Bush "Law": Non-compliance with Clinton's Executive Order *re* Environmental Justice

Citation: Executive Order 12898: Federal Actions to Address Environmental Justice in Minority Populations and Low-Income Populations, February 11, 1994.

Who is hurt by non-compliance with the Executive Order: Minority and low-income populations are hurt by environmental racism especially in regard to Superfund sites.[1] These environmentally hazardous locations vary in their toxic contents, but many contain pollutants and toxins such as lead, mercury, pesticides, chlorinated solvents, Polycholorindated Biphenyls (PCBs), cyanide, benzene, plutonium, uranium and asbestos, among others.[2] Living near these sites causes terrible health hazards such as lung cancer, respiratory problems, severe organ damage, retardation, infertility, birth defects, and more.[3] A disproportionate number of these sites are located in neighborhoods with minorities or people with low-income.[4] In Oakland, CA, one of these open-air sites is located across the street from a playground.[5]

61

What the Executive Order provides: In 1994, Pres. Clinton issued E.O. 12898 aimed at ending environmental racism. This Order said that federal agencies were to make reports as to how they were achieving environmental justice by identifying and addressing, "disproportionately high and adverse human health or environmental effects of [their] programs, policies, and activities on minority populations and low-income populations."

What non-compliance ignores:

U.S. Constitution, General Welfare Clause, Art. I, §8, cl. 1.
U.N. Charter, Preamble.
U.N. Charter, Art. 55 & 56.
International Covenant on Civil and Political Rights (ICCPR), Preamble.
ICCPR, Art. 2(1).
ICCPR, Art. 7.
ICCPR, Art. 23(1).
ICCPR, Art. 24(1).
ICAT, Art. 16(1).
ICERD, Art. 5.

Bills proposed to enforce compliance:

H.R. 1972: Community Environmental Equity Act (introduced 4/19/07); sponsored by Rep. Nydia Velazquez (D-NY) with 4 cosponsors.

S. 2549: Environmental Justice Renewal Act (introduced 1/23/08); sponsored by Sen. Hilary Clinton (D-NY) with 4 cosponsors.

H.R. 5132: Environmental Justice Renewal Act (introduced 1/23/08); sponsored by Rep. Hilda Solis (D-CA) with 4 cosponsors.

H.R. 1103: Environmental Justice Act of 2007 (introduced 2/15/07); sponsored by Rep. Hilda Solis (D-CA) with 54 cosponsors.

S. 642: Environmental Justice Act of 2007 (introduced 2/15/07); sponsored by Sen. Richard Durbin (D-IL) with 4 cosponsors.

H.R. 4652: Environmental Justice Access and Implementation Act of 2007 (introduced 12/13/07); sponsored by Rep. Alcee Hastings (D-FL) with 38 cosponsors.

H.R. 5896: Environmental Justice Enforcement Act of 2008 (introduced 4/24/08); sponsored by Rep. Hilda Solis (D-CA) with 1 cosponsor.

S. 2918: Environmental Justice Enforcement Act of 2008 (introduced 4/24/08); sponsored by Sen. Robert Menéndez (D-NJ) with 3 cosponsors.

What Congress can do: In 2009, Congressmembers can reintroduce and pass the above legislation.

See also: Green Action, http://www.greenaction.org/, (8/8/08).

---

[1] National Council of Churches, *African American Church Leaders Pledge Their Support to the Struggle Against Environmental Racism,* http://www.ncccusa.org/news/news21.html, (8/8/08).

[2] *Superfund,* http://www.pollutionissues.com/Re-Sy/Superfund.html, (8/8/08).

[3] International Joint Commission, *Hazardous Waste Sites and Human Health, Health Effects Review,* Aug. 1999, http://www.ijc.org/rel/boards/hptf/pdf/vol3s3e.pdf (8/8/08).

[4] Supra, Note 1.

[5] Rev. Daniel A. Buford, *San Francisco Bay Area Toxic Triangle Twenty Four Year Timeline,* July 31, 2008 (MCLI).

Bush "Law": 2006 NASA Memo Canceling the DSCOVR Satellite Project

Citation: National Aeronautics and Space Administration Authorization Act of 2008 (H.R. 6063).

Who is hurt by this "law": This decision by NASA officials inhibits the collection of information that many scientists claim is vital to the debate over Global Warming. As a result, U. S. citizens and peoples around the world could be subjected to the adverse effects of Global Warming should Congress and NASA remain inactive on the issue.

What the "law" provides: In January 2006, NASA officially canceled the launch and operation of the already purchased and completed satellite DSCOVR, citing the "competing priorities" of their various projects.[1] DSCOVR satellite has equipment capable of taking measurements vital to testing atmospheric conditions that are consistent with global warming: the albedo levels of Earth.

63

The National Academy of Sciences declared this a "strong and vital" project. For $100,000,000, NASA developed and completed construction of DSCOVR. But NASA has kept DSCOVR grounded at a cost of $1,000,000 a year for over two years, even though France and Ukraine offered to purchase DSCOVR or launch it for free. "Dr. Robert L. Park, professor of physics at the University of Maryland, is... blunt: 'Not knowing [the information it could provide] may kill us.'"[2]

As of January 2006, NASA and the Bush appointees who head it declined to enumerate their reasons for the cancellation of this project[3], citing "deliberative process privilege" and declaring themselves and their offices exempt from Freedom of Information Act requirements that they release internal documents.

NASA budgetary requests compelled Congress to allow for the scrapping of the DSCOVR project and as of May 2008, Congress complied.

What the "law" ignores:
U.S. Constitution, General Welfare Clause, Art. I, §8, cl. 1.
U.N. Charter, Art. 55(b), 56.
ICCPR, Art. 19(2).

What Congress can do: In 2009, Congress can alter proposed NASA Authorization Act of 2008, sponsored by Rep. Ralph Udall (D-CO), that would require NASA to "develop a plan for the Deep Space Climate Observatory (DSCOVR), including such options as using the parts of the spacecraft in the development and assembly of other science missions, transferring the spacecraft to another agency, reconfiguring the spacecraft for another Earth science mission, establishing a public-private partnership for the mission, and entering into an international cooperative partnership to use the spacecraft for its primary or other purposes." The 2009 bill could deny NASA the option of "using the parts of the spacecraft in the development and assembly of other science missions," and instead make available only those options that would ensure NASA will carry out the launch and utilize DSCOVR to gather more precise and complete albedo data than any other current satellite.

---

[1] Mitchell Anderson, "Free DSCOVR." SEEDMagazine.com. September 2006: http://seedmagazine.com/news/2006/09/free_dscovr.php?page=2
[2] Ibid
[3] National Aeronautics and Space Administration. (July 26, 2007)

"Office of the General Counsel's Reply to Mr. Mitchell Anderson."
Retrieved June 6, 2008, from: http://www.desmogblog.com/sites/
beta.desmogblog.com/files/FIOA%20appeal%20response.pdf

Bush Law: Energy Policy Act of 2005

Citation: Public Law 109-58, 119 Stat. 594.

Who is hurt by this law: This law harms the health of U.S. residents, consumers, and the environment, because it "fails to reduce America's dependence on oil, fails to address the threat of global warming, fails to make any new investments in clean energy, and...fails to help consumers at the gas pump."[1] Anyone who relies on corn as a food source is harmed by the law's call for an increase in the ethanol in gasoline because it drives up global grain prices causing food shortages. The rise in U. S. ethanol production has raised food prices by $47 per person each year at a time when unemployment is rising, with 3,420,000 people receiving unemployment compensation, and inflation-adjusted household income has declined by $1,175 since 2000 while expenses of average families have increased by more than $4,600.[2] People in Mexico are protesting the high prices of corn tortillas, a staple in the local diet.[3]

What the law provides: The law gives $85 billion in tax breaks and subsidies to most types of energy industries, with the largest going to the nuclear and oil industries. It also increases the amount of biofuel in gasoline to 6.1 billion gallons by 2009 and 7.5 billion gallons by 2012, which will create both ethanol shortages and food shortages. In certain circumstances, §§322 and 323 exempt the oil and gas industries from complying with the Safe Drinking Water Act[4] and the Clean Water Act[5]. Sec. 357 allows harmful underwater oil and gas exploration that might lead to drilling off U.S. coastlines. The law also provides $6 billion in incentives to coal plants that produce huge amounts of pollution each year and contribute to global warming.

What the law ignores:

U. S. Constitution, General Welfare Clause, Art. I, §8, cl. 1.

U. N. Charter, Art. 55 & 56.

What Congress can do: In 2009, Congressmembers can: (1) repeal the Energy Policy Act of 2005, and (2) pass legislation that

65

protects the environment while developing sustainable energy

practices without giving subsidies and tax cuts to the nuclear and oil industries.

See also: Sustainable Energy and Economy Network, www.sean.org

---

[1] Summary of Harmful Provisions in the Energy Bill, July 28, 2005, http://www.sierraclub.org/globalwarming/bush_plan/energy bill_bad_provisions7_28_05.pdf, (8/19/08).

[2] Testimony of Elizabeth Warren, Leo Gottlieb Professor, Harvard Law School, at July 24, 2008 hearing of Joint Economic Committee of U. S. Congress. http://www.alternet,org/story/95731 (8/19/08).

[3] Dawn Stover, *Is America Headed for a Food Shortage?*, *Popular Science*, June 6, 2007.

[4] Safe Drinking Water Act, 42 U. S. C. 300f.

[5] Clean Water Act, 33 U. S. C. 26.

Bush "Law": Complex Transformation of U. S. Nuclear Weapons

Citation: National Defense Authorization Act for Fiscal Year 2008, Public Law 110-181.

Who is hurt by this "law": This act will affect the environment and the people living in the United States. The Department of Energy (DOE) is spending billions of dollars that could go for current services. This act will hurt the reputation of the U.S. abroad and increase international tension and hostilities with the proliferation of nuclear weapons.

What the "law" provides: The Bush Administration has proposed a plan called "Complex Transformation"[1] that would refurbish the U.S. Nuclear Weapons Complex at the eight sites around the country that produce and maintain our nuclear weapons. The National Nuclear Security Administration (NNSA) is the semi-autonomous nuclear weapons agency within the DOE. It lays out the agency's vision for the future of U.S. nuclear weapons production, research, and testing complex[2], including extending the life of thousands of nuclear warheads and delivery systems originally designed to fight World War III against the Soviet Union.[3] The Bush Nuclear Posture Review increases the number of contingencies in which nuclear weapons could be

66

employed against non-nuclear states, and expands the list of targets of nuclear warheads. It advocates shifting to a planning and command structure that will make it faster and easier to execute limited nuclear attacks.[4] It seeks securing the future of nuclear weapons production and research by revamping infrastructure and adding capabilities across the complex. If allowed to move forward, this new Bombplex will design new nuclear weapons and resume industrial-scale bomb production.[5]

What the "law" ignores:

U.S. Constitution, Art. I, Sec. 9, cl. 7.

International Court of Justice, July 8, 1996[6] (Unanimously): "There exists an obligation to pursue in good faith and bring to a conclusion negotiations leading to nuclear disbarment in all its aspects under strict and effective international control."

Treaty on the Non-Proliferation of Nuclear Weapons (NPT)[7] Art. VI: "Each of the Parties...undertakes to pursue negotiations in good faith on effective measures relating to cessation of the nuclear arms race at an early date and to nuclear disarmament, and on a treaty on general and complete disarmament under strict and effective international control."

Strategic Offensive Reduction Treaty (SORT)[8] agreement between U.S. and Russia to limit nuclear arsenal to 1700–2200 operationally deployed warheads each (signed in Moscow May 24, 2002). SORT came into force June 1, 2003 after the Bush-Putin ratification in St. Petersburg; expires Dec. 31, 2012. (Either party can withdraw on 3 months written notice.)

U.N. Charter, Art. 2.4.

Bills proposed to repeal the "law":

S.1914: Nuclear Policy and Posture Review Act of 2007: Prohibits the appropriation or availability of funds for the Reliable Replacement Warhead Program for FY2008-FY2010 until reports on the above reviews have been submitted to Congress. (introduced 8/1/07); sponsored by Sen. Dianne Feinstein (D-CA) with 9 cosponsors.

What Congress can do: In 2009, Congress can pass S.1914; can limit funding for the Complex Transformation in favor of nuclear disarming by the U.S. and other countries; pass a resolution reiterating the U.S. commitment to the NPT; seek clear objectives that produce greater accountability on the research, testing, and proliferation of nuclear weapons by the U. S.; republish the International Court of Justice opinion in the Federal Register.

[1] "Complex Transformation" formerly known as "Complex 2030".

[2] http://www.ananuclear.org/Issues/NuclearWeapons/ComplexTransformation/tabid/94/Default.aspx#

[3] http://www.nrdc.org/nuclear/insecurity/execsum.asp

[4] *Ibid.*

[5] http://www.ananuclear.org/Issues/NuclearWeapons/ComplexTransformation

[6] General List No. 95, Advisory Opinion, The Legality of the Threat or Use of Nuclear Weapons.

[7] Treaty to reduce & limit spread of nuclear weapons signed by the U.S., July 1, 1968.

[8] U.S. Senate, Mar. 6, 2003, SORT Resolution of Ratification, T.Doc. 107-8: the 'Moscow Treaty'.

Bush Law: Consolidated Appropriations Act Cutting Funding for EPA Libraries

Citation: FY 2008 Consolidated Appropriations Act (H.R. 2764).

Who is hurt by this law: The closure of these vital EPA libraries hurts both those public servants and private enterprises who rely on access to the important environmental data housed exclusively in these libraries to engage in environmentally-sound practices.

What the law provides: On September 13, 2006, the Environmental Protection Agency issued Notification of Closure of three of its ten regional libraries to the public [FRL-8221-3], citing the growing trend toward electronic information and declining physical visits[1], sought a $2,000,000 budget cut, despite the fact that the EPA was created for the "...gathering of information, and the use of this information in strengthening environmental protection programs and recommending policy changes." To realize the ends for which it was created, the EPA had established a national library system to provide extensive collections of data and scientific information made available by governmental agencies and private industries to aid in policy-making, private development, and public projects.[2] The Government Accountability Office says these services have proved essential to the administration of environmental policy, promotion of responsible private practices, and assisting in environmental research.[3] In the face of widespread criticism over these library closures[4], the EPA issued its "National Library Network Report to Congress" on March 28, 2008 with a commitment to "re-establish on-site libraries for EPA staff and members of the public in Region [5, 6, and 7]; and at the EPA

Headquarters Repository and Chemical Library in Washington...
on or before September 30, 2008."[5] In actuality, the library in
Region 5 will be in a facility less than 1/10th its original size;
staff across the national library system have been reduced so
the libraries will have only single workstations, and much of the
original texts and materials will be unavailable to the public.[6]
September 2007 Congress passed the FY 2008 Consolidated
Appropriations Act (H.R. 2764) which "includes $1,000,000
above the request to restore the network of EPA libraries recently
closed or consolidated" and not the $2,000,000 desired by the
Senate. EPA "is directed to submit a report to the Committees on
Appropriations" on its restorative actions within 90 days."[7]

What the law ignores:

U.S. Constitution, General Welfare Clause, Art. I, §8, cl. 1.
U.S. Constitution, First Amendment.
U.N. Charter, Art. 55(b), 56.
ICCPR, Art. 19(2).

What Congress can do:

In 2009, Congress can require EPA to restore their libraries to their
1/1/06 levels and to fund the digitalizing of the library materials
while retaining the physical libraries.

---

[1] EPA. (September 20, 2006), Notification of Closure of the EPA
Headquarters Library

[2] U.S. EPA. (July 9, 1970). Reorganization Plan No. 3: "Plans to Establish
the Environmental Protection Agency and the National Oceanic and
Atmospheric Administration."

[3] Government Accountability Office. (February 2008). "Environmental
Protection: EPA Needs to Ensure That Best Practices and Procedures
Are Followed When Making Further Changes to Its Library Network."
Retrieved June 6, 2008, from http://www.peer.org/docs/epa/08_13_3_
gao_report_on_library_closures.pdf

[4] Christopher Lee. "Budget Cut Would Shutter EPA Libraries."
Washington Post, May 15, 2006: http://www.washingtonpost.com/wp-
dyn/content/article/2006/05/14/AR2006051400772.html

[5] EPA. (March 26, 2008). "EPA National Library Network Report to
Congress."

[6] Carol Goldberg. "Closed EPA Libraries to Return in Lavatory-Sized
Spaces." PEER, May 21, 2008: http://www.peer.org?news/news_
id.php?row_id=1051

[7] Barbie Keiser. "EPA Libraries: Where Do They Stand Now?" News
Breaks. February 12, 2007: http://newsbreaks.infotoday.com/nbReader.
asp?ArticleId=19226

HEALTH CARE

Bush Law: 2003 Revisions of Health Insurance Portability and Accountability Act (HIPAA) of 1996

Citation: Standards for Privacy of Individually Identifiable Health Information (45 C.F.R. §164.512 and §164.520).

Who is hurt by this "law": Every person in the U.S. who has, or expects to have, any health problems and who has health insurance, long-term care services, or medical savings accounts is endangered by this Act.[1]

What the "law" provides: In 2003 the Bush Administration's Department of Health and Human Services (HHS) issued addendums to the HIPAA: §§ 45 C.F.R. 164.512 and 45 C.F.R. 164.520: "A covered entity may use or disclose protected health information without the written consent or authorization of the individual as described in §§ 164.506 and 164.508, respectively... A covered entity may disclose protected health information for the public health activities and purposes described in this paragraph ..." New provisions allow for the release of private information to employers,[2] commercial researchers,[3] and law enforcement agencies,[4] all without notifying the concerned individual or

70

acquiring a warrant,[5] and depriving the individual of the right to sue providers when they feel their medical information has been mishandled. The only significant redress for patients is the ability to file a complaint against companies to the HHS, which itself will be expected to uphold only voluntary compliance procedure concerning the safeguards surrounding medical information.[6]

What the "law" ignores:

U.S. Constitution, General Welfare Clause, Art. I, §8, cl. 1.
U.S. Constitution, Fifth Amendment.
U.S. Constitution, Fourth Amendment.
U.S. Constitution, Ninth Amendment.
ICCPR, Art. 23, §1.
ICCPR, Art. 24, §2.

What Congress can do: In 2009, Congress can repeal these revisions to HIPAA, reasserting through legislation the right of each individual to maintain the confidentiality of their health information and to have control over the dissemination of that information. This would reinstate medical information security for the individual and limit the encroachment of law enforcement and insurance and pharmaceutical groups on these rights.

---

[1] *See* "Bush Seeks to Loosen HIPAA Rules." HR.BLR.com. March 22, 2002. Retrieved on June, 29, 2008 from <http://hr.blr.com/news.aspx?id=4103>.

[2] §45 C.F.R. 164.512 (D)(iv)

[3] §45 C.F.R. 164.512 (h)(i)

[4] §45 C.F.R. 164.512 (6)(i)

[5] "Government Access to Personal Medical Information." www.aclu.org. May, 30, 2003. Retrieved on June 29, 2008 from <http://www.aclu.org/privacy/medical/15222res20030530.html#_ednref11>

[6] "HIPAA Enforcement Brings No Fines." HR.BLR.com. June 7, 2006. Retrieved on June 29, 2008 from <http://hr.blr.com/news.aspx?id=18491>.

Bush "Law": New Freedom Commission on Mental Health (TMAP) and Subsequent Reports

Citation: Executive Order #13263 of April 29, 2002.

Who is hurt by this "law:" Should the recommendations of the New Freedom Commission be implemented in full, the sanctity of the relationship between a patient and a doctor shall be forever violated, as the influences of major pharmaceutical companies shall become an intrusive third-party in that dynamic, and motivations for profit will supersede the delivery of quality healthcare.

What the "law" provides: On April 29, 2002, Bush issued Executive Order #13263 that established the President's New Freedom Commission on Mental Health "to improve America's mental health service delivery system for individuals with serious mental illness and children with serious emotional disturbances."[1] In the Final Report issued by the Commission on July 22, 2003, the Commission touted the Texas Medication Algorithm Project (TMAP) as an ideal means "to ensure quality care for people with serious mental illnesses by developing, applying, and evaluating medication algorithms."[2] In response to this report, Pres. Bush ordered more than 25 federal agencies to develop and implement plans based on these recommendations.[3] Since the development of TMAP in 1997, its implementation has been controversial as it was funded by Johnson & Johnson, Janssen, Pfizer, Eli Lilly, and GlaxoSmithKline,[4] many of which were major donors to the Bush Election Campaigns of 2000 and 2004.[5] Many of these companies have realized record-breaking profits through the implementation of TMAP, as the project "promotes the use of newer, more expensive antidepressants and antipsychotic drugs,"[6] while studies in both the U. S. and UK suggest that "using the older drugs first makes sense. There's nothing in the labeling of the newer atypical antipsychotic drugs that suggests they are superior in efficacy to haloperidol [an older "typical" antipsychotic]. There has to be an enormous amount of unnecessary expenditures for the newer drugs."[7] See, e.g., the case of Allen Jones, a former employee with the Pennsylvania Office of the Inspector General, who on divulging to the media that officials responsible for implementing the plan in Pennsylvania had received money and other perks from these drug companies, was terminated from his position in the OIG.[8]

What the "law" ignores:

U.S. Constitution, General Welfare Clause, Art. I, §8, cl. 1.
ICCPR, Art. 23, §1.

What Congress can do: In 2009, Congress can explicitly deny funding to any state health program that adheres to the TMAP structure and Congress can prohibit outright the implementation of TMAP.

---

[1] "President's New Freedom Commission on Mental Health." George W. Bush. Federal Register, Vol. 67, No. 86. May 3, 2002. Retrieved on July 9, 2008 from http://www.mentalhealthcommission.gov/reports/FinalReport/ExecOrder.htm.

[2] "Goal 5: Excellent Mental Health Care is Delivered and Research is Accelerated." New Freedom Commission on Mental Health Final Report. July 22, 2003. Retrieved on July 9, 2008 from http://www.mentalhealth commission.gov/reports/FinalReport/FullReport-06.htm.

[3] Jeanne Lenzer. "Bush Plans to Screen Whole US Population for Mental Illness." British Medical Journal, retrieved on July 9, 2008 from http://www.bmj.com/cgi/content/full/328/7454/1458.

[4] Dani Veracity. "TMAP, Medication Algorithm Horrors, and the Drugging of Our Children." February 21, 2006. Retrieved on July 9, 2008 from http://www.naturalnews.com/018715.html

[5] supra note 4.

6http://www.interventionmag.com/cms/modules.php?op=modload&na me=News&file=article&sid=830

[7] supra note 3.

[8] http://psychrights.org/Drugs/AllenJonesTMAPJanuary20.pdf

Bush Law: Medicare Prescription Drug Improvement and Modernization Act of 2003 (MMA)[1]

Citation: Public Law 108-173.

Who is hurt by this law:

I. Every person living in the U.S. and future generations will be paying for this law that will increase the growing deficit. In 2007, Medicare provided health care coverage for 43 million people. Enrollment is expected to reach 77 million by 2031, when the baby boom generation is fully eligible.[2] The Medicare program will be subject to draconian cuts and more privatization. The elderly, disabled, children and low-income families will receive reductions in benefits and increases in Part B and D premiums, or, ultimately, a cap on the amount the government will pay per beneficiary, regardless of that person's health care needs.[3] Former Comptroller General David Walker claims that: "The prescription drug bill was probably the most fiscally irresponsible piece of legislation since the 1960s... The problem with Medicare... is people keep living longer, and medical costs keep rising at twice the rate of inflation. But instead of dealing with the problem, he says, the president and the Congress made things much worse in Dec. 2003, when they expanded the Medicare program to include prescription drug coverage. If nothing changes, the federal government's not gonna be able to do much more than pay interest on the mounting debt and some entitlement benefits. It won't have money left for anything else – national defense, homeland security, education, you name it."[4] The Government Accountability Office declares: "In the short term, sponsors' decisions regarding MMA options resulted in benefits relatively unchanged, but over the longer term the effect is unclear."[5]

II. Older, poorer, and sicker individuals—who either do not make enough to benefit from the tax incentives of HSAs, cannot afford the high out-of-pocket costs necessary to enroll in HSAs, or both—will remain in traditional, low-deductible insurance plans.[6] Therefore, isolating the sickest and poorest in one pool—without the youngest, healthiest, and wealthiest to help balance costs—will result in substantial increases in premiums for the population most at risk and least able to pay.[7]

What the law provides:

I. On December 8, 2003, Bush signed MMA "providing seniors and individuals with disabilities with a prescription drug benefit, more choices, and better benefits under Medicare."[8] It was only with the Bush Administration's proposed long-term budget of $534 billion over ten years and guarantees that the budget would remain small and the system would not be expansionary of governmental influences in the health care industry that many members of Congress voted for this bill. Soon after the signing, that figure jumped to $1.2 trillion.[9] The law specifically forbids the federal government to negotiate discounted prescription costs for seniors with pharmaceutical companies.[10]

II. MAA also created Health Savings Accounts (HSAs), designed to help individuals save for future qualified medical and retiree health expenses on a tax-free basis. HSAs offer tax benefits for people who purchase insurance policies with high deductibles. To qualify for the HSA tax break, the policy must have a deductible of at least $1,000 (for an individual) or $2,000 (for a family), but they may run as high as $10,200.

An HSA is a tax-preferred savings account. Deposits into the HSA may be deducted from income for federal income taxes. A maximum of $2,600 (for an individual) or $5,150 (for a family) can be deducted in one year. The tax deductible contributions may be placed into an HSA by an individual, an employer, or both.

Withdrawals from health savings accounts that are used to pay for out-of pocket health care costs are tax-free, while withdrawals for non-medical uses are subject to income tax and a 10 percent penalty for people under 65. Money not used can be rolled over from one year to the next. People over 65 may withdraw money from their accounts—for any reason—without facing the penalty. Money in the accounts can be invested in stocks and bonds without incurring tax on the earnings.[11] HSAs became available on January 1, 2004, and have continued to gain popularity with employers.[12]

What the law ignores:

U.S. Constitution, General Welfare Clause, Art. I, §8, cl. 1.
U.S. Constitution, Ninth Amendment.
ICCPR, Art. 23, §1.
ICCPR, Art. 24, §2.
ICERD, Art. 5(e)(iv).

What Congress can do: In 2009, Congress can pass the proposed bills to amend MMA:

H.R.4: Medicare Prescription Drug Price Negotiation Act of 2007: Introduced 1/5/07; by Rep. John Dingell (D-MI) with 198 cosponsors: To amend part D of title XVIII of the Social Security Act to require the Secretary of Health and Human Services to negotiate lower covered part D drug prices on behalf of Medicare beneficiaries.

S.1576: Minority Health Improvement and Health Disparity Elimination Act: Introduced 6/7/07, by Sen. Edward Kennedy (D-MA) with 19 cosponsors: To amend the Public Health Service Act to improve the health and healthcare of racial and ethnic minority groups.

H.R.3333: (identical to S. 1576; introduced 8/2/07; by Rep. Jesse Jackson (D-IL) with 67 cosponsors).

H.R. 3234: HSA Improvement and Expansion Act of 2007: Introduced 7/31/07 by Rep. Eric Cantor (R-VA) with 48 cosponsors.

---

[1] For a copy of MMA see: http://frwebgate.access.gpo.gov/cgi-bin/getdoc.cgi?dbname=
108_cong_public_laws&docid=f:publ173.108.pdf

[2] http://www.cms.hhs.gov/ReportsTrustFunds/

[3] http://www.medicareadvocacy.org/Reform_07_

05.03.45PercentRule.htm

[4] Andy Court. "U.S. Heading For Financial Trouble?" CBS News, July 8, 2007. http://www.cbsnews.com/stories/2007/03/01/60minutes/main2528226_page2.shtml

[5] "Majority of Sponsors Continue to Offer Prescription Drug Coverage and Chose the Retiree Drug Subsidy." United States Government Accountability Office, May 2007. http://www.gao.gov/new.items/do7572.pdf

[6] http://www.aflcio.org/issues/healthcare/hsa.cfm

[7] http://www.familiesusa.org/assets/pdfs/Bad-ideas_HSAs.pdf

[8] "Medicare Modernization Update." Department of Health and Human Services. http://www.cms.hhs.gov/mmaupdate.

[9] Mike Allen and Ceci Connolly. "Medicare Drug Benefit May Cost $1.2 Trillion." Washington Post. February 9th, 2005. http://www.washingtonpost.com/wp-dyn/articles/A9328-2005Feb8.html.

[10] Under Part D, beneficiaries will be able to access limited prescription drug benefits by contracting with private health plans. Beneficiaries will be subject to formulary restrictions and will be required to pay substantial costs out-of-pocket, including premiums, a deductible, co-insurance, and all costs incurred within a "doughnut hole," as well as the entire costs of drugs not included on their plan's formulary. http://www.medicareadvocacy.org/PrescDrugs_DollarThresholdsIn2003Act.htm

[11] Supra note 7.

[12] Survey on Health Savings Accounts (Washington: Mercer Human Resource Consulting, April 2004).

Bush-Cheney Order: Deleting Testimony on Climate Change

Citation: Testimony before Senate Committee on Environment and Public Works by the Director of the Center for Disease Control and Prevention: "Climate Change and Public Health"- October 23, 2007.[1]

Who is hurt by this order: Members of Congress who must vote to fund the operations and activities of executive agencies while not getting information produced by them for political reasons are hurt by this order.

Everyone will be affected by lack of Congressional information on the dangers of climate change leading to inaction, inadequate action, or unwise action. Specifically, everyone is hurt who is already concerned about climate change, everyone doing research on this subject, and ultimately everyone who will be affected by climate change.

What the redaction order provides:
The Office of the Vice President (OVP) claimed that the testimony was edited because of "an overall lack of precision." Sen. Barbara Boxer (D-CA) claims the real motivations of the Executive in this case have been attempts to prevent enforcement of the regulations required by the Clean Air Act.[2]

The Council on Environmental Quality (CEQ) and the OVP required deletions from testimony of the following language:

"Climate change is anticipated to alter the frequency, timing, intensity, and duration of extreme weather events, such as hurricanes and floods. The health effects of these extreme weather events range from loss of life... to indirect effects such as loss of home, large-scale population displacement, damage to sanitation infrastructure.., interruption of food production, damage to the health-care infrastructure, and psychological problems such as post traumatic stress disorder." "Altered weather patterns resulting from climate change are likely to affect the distribution and incidence of food- and water-borne diseases." "Currently sophisticated models to predict climate and heat exist." "CDC considers climate change a serious public health concern."[3]

What the redaction order ignores:
The Center for Disease Control and Prevention (CDC) is charged with "promot[ing] health and quality of life by preventing and controlling disease, injury, and disability."[4]
U.S. Constitution, Art. 1, Sec. 8, cl. 1.
U.S. Constitution Art. 1, Sec. 8.
U.S. Constitution, Art. II, Sec. 3.
U.N. Charter, Art. 55(b), 56.
ICCPR, Art. 19.1.
ICCPR, Art. 19.2

What Congress can do: In 2009, Congress can pass legislation requiring the full disclosure of the documents and data produced by executive agencies even when it may be critical of their actions in order to prevent the editing of testimony essential to the fulfillment of Congressional duties.

[1] Julilet Eilperin. "Cheney's Staff Cut Testimony on Warming." July 9, 2008. Washington Post. www.washingtonpost.com. Retrieved on July 14, 2008 from <http://www.washingtonpost.com/wp-dyn/content/article/2008/07/08/AR2008070801442_2.html?hpid=moreheadlines&sub=new>.

[2] Id.

[3] Julie Gerberding. "Redacted-Climate Change and Public Health." October, 23, 2007. Center for Disease Control and Prevention. Retrieved on July 14, 2008 from <http://www.scienceprogress.org/wp-content/uploads/2007/10/Gerberding_testimony_final.pdf>.

[4] CDC's Mission. Center for Disease Control and Prevention. www.cdc.gov. Retrieved on July 14, 2008 from <"http://www.cdc.gov/about/>.

Bush "Law": Model State Emergency Health Powers Act (MSEHPA)

Citation: Model State Emergency Health Powers Act, www.publichealthlaw.net

Who is hurt by the "law": After 9/11/2001, the U.S. Department of Health and Human Services announced its support for model state legislation providing for the streamlining of health services in the wake of such national emergencies as bioterrorist attacks. On December 21, 2001 through several subsidiaries including the Centers for Disease Control and the Center for Law and the Public's Health at Georgetown and Johns Hopkins Universities, HHS produced and released the final version of the Model State Emergency Health Powers Act. The "model act" contains provisions allowing for the indefinite isolation of individuals and forcing medications on them. The draft grants very broad police powers to public-health authorities, and would exempt from liability those carrying out the orders.[1] Under the broad definition of "public health emergency" in MSEHPA, some harmless threat such as an influenza outbreak could qualify as an "emergency" and result in the execution of these powers. According to the Center for Law and the Public's Health: "As of July 15, 2006,... thirty-eight states and DC have passed a total of 66 bills or resolutions that include provisions from or closely related to the Act."[2]

What the "law" provides: Model State Emergency Health Powers Act: [3]

Art. IV, Sec. 401: "A state of public health emergency may be declared by the Governor upon the occurrence of a public health emergency...the governor may act to declare a public health emergency without consulting with the public health authority... when the situation calls for prompt and timely action."

Art. V, Sec. 602: "During a state of public health emergency the public health authority may perform physical examinations and/or tests as necessary for the diagnosis or treatment of individuals...the public health authority may isolate or quarantine any person whose refusal of medical examination or testing results in uncertainty regarding whether he or she has been exposed to or is infected with a contagious or possibly contagious disease..."

Art. V, Sec. 604, part (a): "The public health authority may also establish and maintain places of isolation and quarantine, and set rules and make orders. Failure to obey these rules, orders, or provisions shall constitute a misdemeanor."

Art. V, Sec. 604, part (c): "Persons subject to isolation or quarantine shall obey the public health authority's rules and orders; and shall not go beyond the isolation or quarantine premises. Failure to obey these provisions shall constitute a misdemeanor."

What the "law" ignores:

U.S. Constitution, General Welfare Clause, Art. I, §8, cl. 1.
U.S. Constitution, Art. I, Sec. 9, cl. 1. Habeas Corpus.
U.S. Constitution, Fourth Amendment.
U.S. Constitution, Fifth Amendment.
U.S. Constitution, Sixth Amendment.
U.S. Constitution, Eighth Amendment.
U.S. Constitution, Ninth Amendment.
U.S. Constitution, Tenth Amendment.
U.S. Constitution, Fourteenth Amendment.
ICCPR, Art. 23, Section 1.

What Congress can do: In 2009, Congress can cease funding the Center for Law and the Public Health to stop the promotion and dissemination of this "model" act. It can disavow the act's recommendations and acknowledge the breach of constitutional protections that this "model" act abets. It can pass a resolution urging all states that have adopted provisions of MSEHPA to reconsider and repeal them.

---

[1] "CDC and Public Health Academians Propose Mandatory Vaccination and Treatment for 'Infectious Diseases.'" Institute for Health Freedom. www.forhealthfreedom.org. Retrieved on 6/17/2008 from <http://www.forhealthfreedom.org/Publications/Informed/StateHealthPowersAct.html>.

[2] "Model State Public Health Laws-MSEHPA" The Center for Law and the Public Health. www.publichealthlaw.net. Retrieved on 6/17/2008 from <http://www.publichealthlaw.net/Resources/Modellaws.htm#MSEHPA>.

Bush Law: Deficit Reduction Act of 2005 (DRA)

Citation: 42 U.S.C. 1305.

Who is hurt by this law: The Deficit Reduction Act (DRA) targets non-citizens and perpetuates the racial disparities of healthcare access. The DRA citizenship documentation requirement creates delay and difficulty for women who lack such documentation to secure it in time to access time-sensitive prenatal care through Medicaid.[1] In the years since the law was enacted, eligible, long-standing resident immigrants have been deterred from enrolling in Medicaid because they believe they must produce proof of citizenship, rather than merely proof of legal status, in order to qualify. It is more likely that people of color will be unable to meet the premium and cost-sharing requirements authorized by the DRA and effectively be denied access to health care as a result. By 2015, the Congressional Budget Office estimates that the benefit reduction will affect 1.6 million enrollees, many of whom are people of color.[2]

What the law provides: On February 8, 2006, Pres. Bush signed into law the Deficit Reduction Act, imposing the most significant set of changes to Medicaid's coverage structure since its 1965 enactment. The Act is expected to generate $39 billion in federal entitlement reductions over the 2006 to 2010 period and $99 billion over the 2006 to 2015 period.[3] Section 6037 specifically prohibits "Medicaid assistance to an individual who declares he or she is a U.S. citizen unless one example of specified kinds of documentary evidence of citizenship or nationality is presented."[4]

The Congressional Budget Office (CBO) estimates that the DRA will reduce federal spending by $11.5 billion over the five year period and by $43.2 billion over the next ten years from Medicaid, the program that partners with states to provide health coverage and long-term care assistance to over 39 million people in low-income families and 12 million elderly and disabled people, to fill in gaps in Medicare coverage, and to support safety-net providers.[5]

What the law ignores:

U.S. Constitution, General Welfare Clause, Art. I, §8, cl. 1.
U.N. Charter, Preamble.
ICAT, Preamble.
ICCPR, Art. 2, 12(3), 23(1), 24(1), and 26.
ICERD, Art. 1(2)(3), 2, and 5(e)(iv).

What Congress can do: In 2009, Congress can vote to amend DRA and implement the following bills:

S.909: Introduced 3/15/07; sponsored by Sen. Jeff Bingaman (D-NM) with 9 cosponsors: To amend title XIX (Medicaid) of the Social Security Act to permit states, at their option, to require certain individuals to present satisfactory documentary evidence of citizenship or nationality for Medicaid eligibility.

H.R.1878: (identical to S.909; introduced 4/17/2007 by Rep. Corrine Brown (D-FL)).

S.1576: Minority Health Improvement and Health Disparity Elimination Act: Introduced 6/7/07; by Sen. Edward Kennedy (D-MA) with 19 cosponsors: To amend the Public Health Service Act to improve the health and healthcare of racial and ethnic minority groups.

H.R.3333: (identical to S. 1576; introduced 8/2/07 by Rep. Jesse Jackson (D-IL) with 67 cosponsors).

See also: http://www.kff.org/medicaid/upload/7465.pdf

---

[1] www2.ohchr.org/english/bodies/cerd/docs/ngos/usa/USHRN29.doc

[2] The Kaiser Commission on Medicaid and the Uninsured

[3] http://www.kff.org/medicaid/upload/7465.pdf

[4] http://frwebgate.access.gpo.gov/cgibin/getdoc.cgi?dbname=109_cong_public_laws&docid=f:publ171.109.pdf

[5] Supra, note 3.

Bush Law: Partial Birth Abortion Ban Act of 2003

Citation: 18 U.S.C. 1531.

Who is hurt by this law: The wording in the title "Partial Birth Abortion" Ban Act (PBABA) of 2003, promotes the negative impression on women that the medical procedure is an inhumane abortion action. By allowing the law to use the term "partial birth abortion" so broadly it could be interpreted to outlaw a variation of dilation and evacuation (D&E), by far the most common and safest method of second-trimester abortion (which is relatively rare itself; not to mention those used for women who have learned via amniocentesis, as late as 20 weeks or more, that they're carrying a fatally abnormal fetus).[1] Doctors and patients are negatively affected by PBABA because it interferes with doctor-patient confidentiality. It affects all patients because of the political intrusion on our most private decisions in medical care. More specifically, the ban will affect the right of women to make autonomous choices about their body.[2] PBABA fails to make any exception in the ban when a woman's health is at stake, which violates established constitutional protections that have been in place for 30 years.[3] In response to PBABA, doctor's are avoiding any chance of partially delivering a live fetus, so they are injecting fetuses with lethal drugs before procedures even though it poses a slight risk to the woman and offers her no medical benefit.[4] PBABA is having an impact on medical education: medical students and nursing students are no longer invited to watch later-term abortions, for fear one might misinterpret the procedure and lodge a criminal complaint.[5]

What the law provides: In November 5, 2003, Bush signed into law the Partial Birth Abortion Ban Act (PBABA) to ban a specific abortion procedure used in a limited number of midterm abortions.[6] The medical term for the rare procedure is known as "Intact D & X procedure" (Dilation and Extraction) which may be used in the second trimester.[7] It refers to a process of collapsing the skull with suctioning and delivering the fetus intact. It is rarely done on a live fetus.[8] PBABA provides that a physician who "knowingly performs a partial-birth abortion and thereby kills a human fetus shall be fined under this title or imprisoned not more than 2 years, or both."

In June 28, 2000, the U.S. Supreme Court struck down a similar abortion ban on the ground that it did not contain an exception for

82

the health of the woman, an exception long deemed constitutionally necessary.[9] On April 18, 2007, the Supreme Court justices voted 5-4 to affirm the constitutionality of PBABA in the cases of *Gonzales v. Carhart*[10] and *Gonzales v. Planned Parenthood*,[11] banning certain abortion procedures after the first trimester. It was also the first time since the landmark *Roe v. Wade*[12] decision of January 1973, that justices approved an abortion restriction that did not contain an exception for the health of the woman.[13] It does, however, provide an exception to save the woman's life.[14]

What the law ignores:

U.S. Constitution, Preamble.
U.N. Charter, Preamble, Art. 55.
ICCPR, Preamble, Art. 1, 2(1), 3, 9(1), 17, 26.
ICERD, Preamble, Art. 5(e)(iv).

Bills proposed to amend PBABA:

S.1173: Freedom of Choice Act: Declares the policy of the U. S. that every woman has the fundamental right to choose to: (1) bear a child; (2) terminate a pregnancy prior to fetal viability; or (3) after fetal viability when necessary to protect her life or health. Prohibits U.S. state or local governments from: (1) interfering with a woman's right to exercise such choices; or (2) discriminating against the exercise of those rights in regulation or provision of benefits, facilities, services, or information and such prohibition shall apply retroactively. Authorizes an individual aggrieved by a violation of this Act to obtain appropriate relief, against a government entity in a civil action. (introduced 4/19/07); sponsored by Sen. Barbara Boxer (D-CA).

H.R. 1964: Freedom of Choice Act, sponsored by Rep. Jerrold Nadler (D-NY), identical to S.1173.

What Congress can do: In 2009, Congress can uphold a woman's fundamental right to privacy by voting for the above bills.

See also: www.reproductiverights.org

---

[1] http://www.salon.com/mwt/feature/2007/04/19/scotus_ban/index.html

[2] In fact, by age 45, over one-third of American women will have had an abortion. These women represent all racial, ethnic, socioeconomic, political, and religious backgrounds. http://www.prochoice.org/get_involved/pro_choice_proud.html

3 http://www.reproductiverights.org/crt_pba.html

4 http://www.boston.com/yourlife/health/women/articles/2007/08/10/shots_assist_in_aborting_fetuses/?page=1

5 Supra, note 2.

6 The procedure involves very few abortions - about 2,200 out of 1.31 million in 2000, the last year for which numbers are available. http://www.huffingtonpost.com/jim-wallis/abortion-from-symbol-to-_b_46422.html

7 "The Intact D & X procedure was developed for use in late second trimester abortions as a safety precaution for the woman because there is less cervical dilation and less chance of injuring the uterus with an instrument. This method may improve women's chances of having a healthy pregnancy in the future."

8 http://www.abortionconversation.com/faq.php

9 *Stenberg v. Carhart*, 530 U.S. 914 (2000). The Court reaffirmed that any restriction on abortion must contain an exception to protect a woman's life and health. The Court held that because the ban would outlaw the safest and most common methods of abortion in the second trimester, it was an undue burden on women's right to choose abortion.

10 Supreme Court Case No. 05-380, 550 U.S. ___ (2007). http://www.supremecourtus.gov/opinions/06pdf/05-380.pdf

11 Supreme Court Case No. 05-1382, 550 U.S. ___ (2007).

12 410 U.S. 113 (1973).

13 Justice Ginsburg dissent: "Instead of drawing the line at viability, the Court refers to Congress' purpose to differentiate 'abortion and infanticide' based not on whether a fetus can survive outside the womb, but on where a fetus is anatomically located when a particular medical procedure is performed."

14 http://www.washingtonpost.com/wpdyn/content/article/2007/04/18/AR2007041800710.html

HOUSING/MORTGAGE FORECLOSURES

Bush "Law": Lack of Federal Regulation of Banks and Mortgages

Who is hurt by the lack of regulation: In 2007 alone, nearly 971,000 families lost their homes due to mortgage foreclosures. In the second quarter of 2008, U.S. foreclosures were up 121% from 2007's second quarter.[1] Ten banks have failed since the housing crisis began in mid-2007.[2] The mortgage crisis and the bank failures have contributed to the dwindling U.S. economy, which affects even those whose mortgages have not been foreclosed.

U.S. taxpayers, through the Housing and Economic Recovery Act of 2008,[3] are now bailing out lenders Freddie Mac and Fannie Mae, which hold nearly half of all mortgages in the U.S. The chief executive of Freddie Mac, the second largest mortgage lender in the U.S., ignored internal warnings that the company was underwriting loans that were too risky,[4] which shows that there were warning signs that regulators did not know about or ignored.

What the "law" provides: In 1999, Congress passed the Gramm-Leach-Bliley Act,[5] which repealed the Glass-Steagall Act[6] and, in effect, ended many regulations that prevented mergers and allowed banks to engage in a wider range of financial services. In part because of this act, the Bush Administration did not regulate mortgage lenders enough or effectively investigated the growing number of foreclosures. The Federal Deposit Insurance Corporation (FDIC), Federal Reserve Board (the Fed), Department of Treasury, and Securities and Exchange Commission (SEC) are executive agencies that make up the regulation infrastructure that could have prevented the mortgage crisis.

In mid-2008, the Fed imposed new rules so that lenders do not give "state-income" loans, which are loans that allow borrowers to exaggerate their incomes in order to get the loan because they do not have to provide tax documents for verification.[7] If the Fed had these regulations—and others—in place to begin with, the mortgage crisis would not be as bad as it currently is.

What the lack of regulation ignores:

U.S. Constitution, General Welfare Clause, Art. I, §8, cl. 1.

U.N. Charter, Preamble.

U.N. Charter, Art. 55 & 56.

International Covenant on Civil and Political Rights (ICCPR), Preamble.

ICCPR, Art. 12(1): "Everyone lawfully within the territory of a State shall, within that territory, have the right to liberty of movement and freedom to choose his residence."

CCPR, Art. 23(1).

Bills proposed to increase regulation: The 110th Congress has proposed many bills to remedy parts of the subprime mortgage crisis (e.g. S. 2296, H.R. 3813, H.R. 3296), but more comprehensive regulatory legislation may be needed.

What Congress can do: In 2009, Congressmembers can introduce and pass legislation to increase regulations regarding the banking and mortgage lending industries and pass legislation that will require executive agencies to report how they are investigating compliance with banking and mortgage lending regulations.

See also: National Public Radio, *Subprime Mortgages: A Primer,* http://www.npr.org/templates/story/story.php?storyId=9085408, (8/7/08).

---

[1] *U.S. Foreclosures Up 121 Percent in Second Quarter, Houston Business Journal,* July 25, 2008.

[2] Federal Deposit Insurance Corporation, *FDIC: Failed Banks List,* http://www.fdic.gov/bank/individual/failed/banklist.html, (8/7/08).

[3] Public Law 110-289.

[4] Charles Duhigg, *At Freddie Mac, Chief Discarded Warning Signs, New York Times,* Aug. 5, 2008.

[5] Public Law 106-102, 113 Stat. 1338 (1999).

[6] 48 Stat. 162 (1935).

[7] Holden Lewis, *New Federal Reserve Mortgage Rules Affect Subprime Loans, Sarasota Herald Tribune,* July 26, 2008.

HUMAN RIGHTS

Bush "Law": Directive Abolishing Interagency Working Group on Human Rights Treaties and Transfer of Their Authority to the Policy Coordination Committee on Democracy, Human Rights and International Operations

Citation: National Security Presidential Directive 1 [NSPD-1], February 13, 2001.

Who is hurt by this "law": Citizens and residents of the U.S., and people affected by U.S. policies world-wide who feel they are the victims of racial discrimination, cruel or degrading treatment, or are being deprived of other human rights and protections under the Convention on Elimination of Racial Discrimination, Convention Against Torture and other Cruel, Inhuman or Degrading Treatment or Punishment, or the International Covenant on Civil and Political Rights.[1] Activists and researchers who seek to have the U.S. enforce its obligations under the three treaties also are hurt by the change in title and structure and funding of the agency established to file the reports and otherwise work with the three U.N. committees that enforce the three treaties because the late U.S. reports are now considered inadequate and inaccurate.[2]

What the "law" provides: On December 10, 1998, Pres. Clinton issued Executive Order #13107, providing that the U.S. Government "being committed to the protection and promotion of human rights and fundamental freedoms, [shall] respect and implement its obligations under the international human rights treaties to which it is a party, including the ICCPR, the ICAT, and the ICERD."[3] The Executive Order established the Interagency Working Group and charged it with "providing guidance, oversight, and coordination with respect to questions concerning the adherence to and implementation of human rights obligations and related matters."[4] It required all executive departments and agencies to appoint an officer charged with coordinating and implementing this order within their respective departments.[5]

On Feb. 13, 2001, Pres. Bush issued the National Security Presidential Directive 1, abolishing Clinton's human rights implementation system and transferring its responsibilities to the Policy Coordination Committee on Democracy, Human Rights, and International Operations.[6] In 2001, Pres. Bush then appointed Elliot Abrams to head this Committee, after his earlier criminal conviction for his involvement in the Iran/Contra scandal.[7]

Enforcement of these treaties has become one of the Committee's many responsibilities, rather than being the sole responsibility of the earlier Interagency Working Group.[8]

What the "law" ignores

U.S. Constitution, Art. 6, cl. 2.
ICCPR in its entirety.
ICERD in its entirety.
ICAT in its entirety.

What Congress can do: In 2009, Congress can adopt legislation that returns the responsibility of administering these treaties to a single agency and requires all executive agencies to select staff charged with enforcing these treaties and making the required reports on time to the U.N. committees.

---

[1] ICCPR, see text in Appendix.

[2] See Concluding Observations of the Committee on the Elimination of Racial Discrimination: United States of America, May 8, 2008, ICERD/C/USA/CO/6; Conclusions and Recommendations of the Committee against Torture: United States of America, June 25, 2006, ICAT/C/USA/CA/2; Concluding Observations of the human Rights Committee: United Sates of America, Dec. 18, 2006, CCPR/C/USA/CA/Rev.1.

[3] Executive Order 13107. Implementation of Human Rights Treaties. Federal Register/ Vol. 63, No. 240/ Tuesday, December 15, 1998. Retrieved on July 22, 2008 from < http://frwebgate.access.gpo.gov/cgi-bin/getdoc.cgi?dbname=1998_register&docid=fr15de98-110.pdf >.

[4] Id.

[5] Id.

[6] National Security Presidential Directive 1 [NSPD-1]. The White House. February 13, 2001. Retrieved on July 22, 2008 from <http://www.au.af.mil/au/awc/awcgate/whitehouse/nspd-1.htm>.

[7] Abrams is also known for downplaying the brutality of massacres carried out in South America with the assistance of U.S. federal funding and training. See David Corn. "Elliot Abrams: It's Back!" *The Nation*. June 14, 2001. thenation.com. Retrieved on July 21, 2008 from <http://www.thenation.com/doc/20010702/corn>.

[8] Supra, note 3.

88

IMMIGRATION

Bush "Law": Funding and Administrative Support for Massive Immigration Raids

Citation: Homeland Security Act of 2002, Public Law 107-296, 116 Stat. 2135 (2002).

Who is hurt by this "law": On May 12, 2009, Immigration and Customs Enforcement (ICE) conducted the largest single-site raid in its history at a slaughterhouse in Pottsville, Iowa and arrested 390 unauthorized immigrants, shackled them, and then detained them in various jails. Overnight, the town lost 1/3 of its population, local businesses were deserted, and nearly 1/3 of the students in elementary and middle schools were afraid to show up for school the next day, including some born in the U. S. and therefore U. S. citizens.[1] The 306 held for prosecution were told they could either spend 6-8 months in jail awaiting trial on a charge of aggravated identity theft under 18 U.S.C. §1028A, a crime with an additional two-year mandatory minimum sentence, or plead guilty to the lesser charge of "knowingly using a false social security number," which carries at least a five month jail sentence.[2]

Immigrants, employers, and local economies are injured as a result of massive ICE raids across the country that tear apart

89

communities and families, disrupt the workplace, and have disastrous consequences for employers and their businesses.

What the "law" provides: The Homeland Security Act of 2002 created a new cabinet department, the Department of Homeland Security, which now oversees the Coast Guard, the Secret Service, Federal Emergency Management Agency, and various immigration agencies including ICE, an agency concerned with interior enforcement of both customs and immigration. In addition to dealing with foreign goods, ICE locates and arrests or charges people that it suspects are illegally present in the U.S. and represents the government in removal proceedings.[3] In order to enforce immigration law in the interior, ICE conducts raids on homes and workplaces. The very existence of an agency that puts people and goods in the same category is an affront to human dignity according to human rights workers.

What the "law" ignores:

U.S. Constitution, Fourth Amendment.

U.S. Constitution, Fifth Amendment, Due Process Clause.

U.S. Constitution, Fourteenth Amendment, Equal Protection Clause.

U.N. Charter, Preamble.

U.N. Charter, Art. 55 & 56.

International Covenant on Civil and Political Rights (ICCPR), Preamble.

ICCPR, Art. 2(1).

ICCPR, Art. 9(1).

ICCPR, Art. 10(1).

ICCPR, Art. 17(1).

ICCPR, Art. 23(1).

ICCPR, Art. 26.

ICAT, Art. 16(1).

ICERD, Art. 2(1)(2).

ICERD, Art. 5.

What Congress can do: In 2009, Congressmembers can:

Cut the cost of anti-immigrant raids from the ICE budget;

Suspend immigration raids by passing a resolution against them;

Pass legislation to remove ICE from the Department of Homeland Security;

90

Divide ICE so that customs enforcement and immigration enforcement are not carried out by the same agency.

Contributor: Dan Kesselbrenner, National Immigration Project, National Lawyers Guild.

---

[1] Erik Camayd-Freixas, *Interpreting after the Largest ICE Raid in US History: A Personal Account*, 3, June 13, 2008, http://graphics8.nytimes.com/images/2008/07/14/opinion/14ed-camayd.pdf, (7/16/08).

[2] Id at 5.

[3] Aleinikoff, Martin, Motomura, and Fullterton, *Immigration and Citizenship: Process and Policy*, 268-273 *(6th Edition,* Thompson and West, 2008).

Bush Law: Secure Fence Act of 2006

Citation: Public Law 109-367, 120 Stat. 2638.

Who is hurt by this law: Thousands of residents in border regions and hundreds of plants and animals are being hurt by the 700-mile fence along the U.S.-Mexico border being built by the U.S. Many of those with land straddling the border have refused to let officials survey their property. In December 2007, the Department of Homeland Security (DHS) "sent letters to 135 private landowners, municipalities, universities, public utility companies and conservation societies along the border that had turned away surveyors...[and gave them] 30 days to change their minds or face legal action."[1]

This fence also damages the U.S. in foreign public opinion and sends a very negative message to Mexico. The Mexican government has called the fence "xenophobic and disgraceful",[2] and called it "medieval," condemning the "growing harassment" of Mexican migrants and the devastating environmental consequences.[3]

The Real ID Act hurts everyone who favors three equal branches of government by allowing the Secretary of Homeland Security to waive whatever laws he deems are incompatible with building the fence. DHS Secretary, Michael Chertoff, waived 30 environmental and cultural laws in order to speed construction of the fence.[4]

One of these waived laws deals with tribal land. The fence runs through three Native American nations and affects 23 tribes that live in the borderlands and will literally split them in two.[5]

Both the Mexican government and environmental organizations say the fence threatens hundreds of plant species and animals, including endangered Mexican Gray Wolves and Peninsular Bighorn Sheep.[6]

U.S. taxpayers are being injured because the fence itself will cost nearly $49 billion by the time it is completed, not including the cost of acquiring privately-owned land on the border the U.S. government will have to purchase.[7]

What the law provides: Secure Fence Act: §2(a): "In General.— Not later than 18 months after the date of the enactment of this Act, the Secretary of Homeland Security shall take all actions the Secretary determines necessary...to achieve and maintain operational control over the entire international land and maritime borders of the United States, to include...(2) physical infrastructure enhancements to prevent unlawful entry by aliens into the United States and facilitate access to the international land and maritime borders by U.S. Customs and Border Protection,...additional checkpoints, all weather access roads, and vehicle barriers." Real ID Act, §102: "...Notwithstanding any other provision of law, the Secretary of Homeland Security shall have the authority to waive, and shall waive, all laws such Secretary, in such Secretary's sole discretion, determines necessary to ensure expeditious construction of the barriers and roads under this section."

What the law ignores:
U.S. Constitution, General Welfare Clause, Art. I, §8, cl. 2.
U.S. Constitution, Separation of Powers.
U.N. Charter, Preamble.
ICCPR, Art. 2(1).
ICAT, Art. 16(1).

What Congress can do: In 2009, Congressmembers can:

Call expert witnesses to testify in hearings that the fence is an ineffective deterrent to illegal immigration because an estimated 40-50% of unauthorized immigrants enter through legal ports of entry.[8] And despite their awareness of the dangers of border crossing, migrants who are determined to enter the U.S. try repeatedly to do so, eventually entering with a 96% success rate.[9]

Repeal the Secure Fence Act and the Real ID Act §102.

See also: http://notexasborderwall.com

Contributor: Dan Kesselbrenner, National Immigration Project of the National Lawyers Guild.

---

[1] N.C. Aizenman, *Border Fence Would Slice Through Private Land,* Washington Post, Feb. 16, 2008.

[2] Dudley Althaus & James Pinkerton, *Opinions Split on Proposed Border Fence; Many in Mexico and Some in U.S. against House Plan,* Houston Chronicle, Dec. 30, 2005.

[3] Manuel Roig-Franzia, *Mexico Call U.S. Border Fence Severe Threat to Environment, The Washington Post,* Nov. 16, 2007.

[4] Adam Liptak, *Power to Build Border Fence is Above U.S. Law, New York Times,* Apr. 8, 2008.

[5] Rodrigo París, *Border Fence to Divide Three Native American Nations, New America Media,* Oct. 6, 2006.

[6] Haider Rizvi, *Border Fence Could Spell Environmental Disaster, CommonDreams,* Oct. 3, 2006.

[7] Tyche Hendricks, *Study: Price for Border Fence up to $49 Billion, San Francisco Chronicle,* Jan. 8, 2007.

[8] Melanie Mason, *The Border Fence Folly, The New Republic,* June 30, 2008.

[9] Id.

Bush Law: Real ID Act of 2005

Citation: Public Law 109-13.

Who has been hurt by this law: If Congress does not repeal this Act, it will require everyone to have a national identity card by January 1, 2010, which will introduce a number of anti-immigrant measures.[1] These measures will affect every single one of over 37.9 million immigrants in the U.S.[2] DMV clerks will be forced to determine a person's citizenship or immigration status before they can issue drivers licenses or ID cards.[3] This will lead to discrimination at the DMV because clerks will rely on factors such as accents and skin colors in making the decision whether a person needs to show proper immigration documentation. U.S. taxpayers will suffer because they will be paying for a border fence that will do very little to stem illegal border crossings, but will force migrants to cross the border at more dangerous locations and pay higher prices to criminal smugglers.[4] (*see also*: Secure Fence Act of 2005) The law also amends certain provisions of existing immigration law to expand the definition of "terror-related activity" so that family members of those associated with terrorism, but that have no connection themselves, will be at risk for deportation or removal.[5] In asylum cases, immigration judges are now making credibility determinations that involve considering unfair criteria such as demeanor and responsiveness of the witness, two factors which can vary depending on an asylum seeker's ethnic and social background and the background of the immigration judge.[6]

What the law provides: In order for a person to obtain a driver's license or ID card, the states will require valid documentation that the person is a U.S. citizen; or a lawfully admitted alien, an alien with lawful permanent resident status, a refugee or asylum seeker; has a valid visa, a pending application for asylum, a pending application for temporary protected status, has approved deferred status, or a pending application for adjustment (§ 202(c)(2)(A), (B)).

This law ignores:

The right to privacy in the penumbras of the First and Ninth Amendments.

U.S. Constitution, Tenth Amendment: "The powers not delegated to the United States by the Constitution, nor prohibited by it to the States, are reserved to the States respectively, or to the people."

U.N. Charter, Art. 55 and 56.

International Covenant on Civil and Political Rights (ICCPR), Art. 2(1).

ICCPR, Art. 17(1): "No one shall be subjected to arbitrary or unlawful interference with his privacy, family, or correspondence, nor to unlawful attacks on his honour and reputation."

Bills proposed in 2007:

S. 717: Identification Security Enhancement Act of 2007 (introduced 2/28/2007); sponsored by Sen. Daniel Akaka (D-HI) with 7 cosponsors

H.R. 1117: REAL ID Repeal and Identification Security Enhancement Act of 2007 (introduced 2/16/2007); sponsored by Rep. Thomas Allen (D-ME) with 36 cosponsors.

What Congress can do: Congress can reintroduce and pass these bills from 2007 or repeal the Real ID Act of 2005.

See also: National Conference of State Legislatures: http://www.ncsl.org/print/statefed/Real_ID_Impact_Report_FINAL_Sept19.pdf

---

[1] http://www.ncsl.org/print/statefed/Real_ID_Impact_Report_FINAL_Sept19.pdf (6/18/09).

[2] Center for Immigration Studies http://www.cis.org/CurrentNumbers (6/20/09).

[3] http://www.realnightmare.org/about/5/ (6/17/08).

[4] http://www.nilc.org/immspbs/dls/nclr_real-id_talkingpoints_0305.pdf (6/18/08).

[5] http://www.nilc.org/immspbs/dls/nclr_real-id_talkingpoints_0305.pdf (6/18/08).

[6] http://www.visalaw.com/05may1/3may105.html (6/18/08).

Bush "Law": Board of Immigration Appeals Continuing Inadequate Coverage of Asylum Law

Citation: Immigration and Nationality Act (INA) §208(b)(1)(A), 8 U.S.C. §1158(b)(1)(A).

Who is hurt by this "law": Immigrants who are facing deportation and who are deemed to not fit within the current definition of "refugee" under INA §101(a)(42)(A) are hurt. In particular, gender-related persecution is not being held by the courts as "persecution" under the definition because women are not considered a "social group" under the definition.[1] There are many women in the U.S. who may be harmed if they return to their native countries, but they are denied relief under the INA because the statute is too narrowly tailored.

Courts have also been ruling that the gender-related persecution practice of female genital cutting mutilation (FGM) is not grounds for relief under existing asylum law. The Board of Immigration Appeals (BIA) in *Matter of A-T*,[2] denied protection to Alima Traore, who was subjected to FGM as a child and fears a forced marriage if she were sent back to Mali. The BIA ignored that Ms. Traore continues to endure the consequences of her genital cutting, including ongoing medical, psychological, and sexual problems. The BIA ruled that past FGM is generally not a basis for asylum because it happens to a woman only once, and is therefore not a "continuing harm." The BIA had previously recognized forced reproductive sterilization, which also happens only once, as a permanent and continuing harm. Contrary to international law, the BIA also rejected Ms. Traore's forced marriage claim, characterizing the practice as harmless family tradition rather than persecution.

What the "law" provides: Under the INA, the definition of "refugee" is "...any person who is outside any country of such person's nationality...and who is unable or unwilling to return to, and is unable or unwilling to avail himself or herself of the protection of that country because of persecution or a well-founded fear of persecution on account of race, religion, nationality, membership in a particular social group, or political opinion..."[3]

What the "law" ignores:

U.S. Constitution, General Welfare Clause, Art. I, §8, cl. 1.

U.N. Charter, Preamble.

U.N. Charter, Art. 55 & 56.

ICCPR, Preamble.

ICCPR, Art. 2(1).

ICCPR, Art. 3: "The States Parties to the present Covenant undertake to ensure the equal right of men and women to the enjoyment of all civil and political rights set forth in the present Covenant."

ICCPR, Art. 23(1).

ICCPR, Art. 23(3): "No marriage shall be entered into without the free and full consent of the intending spouses."

ICCPR, Art. 24(1).

ICCPR, Art. 26: "All persons are equal before the law and are entitled without any discrimination to the equal protection of the law. In this respect, the law shall prohibit any discrimination and guarantee to all persons equal and effective protection against discrimination on any ground such as race, colour, sex, language, religion, political or other opinion, national or social origin, property, birth or other status."

ICAT, Art. 3(1): "No State Party shall expel, return ("refouler" or extradite a person to another State where there are substantial grounds for believing that he would be in danger or being subjected to torture."

ICAT, Art. 16(1).

ICERD, Art. 5.

What Congress can do: In 2009, Congressmembers can:

Pass legislation that amends the INA to specify that "women" qualify as a "social group" under the definition.

Pass legislation that ensures that FGM, either past or future, is grounds for asylum relief.

Join the bi-partisan sign-on effort, sponsored by Sen. Olympia Snowe (R-ME) and Sen. Carl Levin (D-MI), that requests that the Attorney General reconsider the outrageous denial of protection to Ms. Traore.

See also: World Health Organization, http://www.who.int/topics/female_genital_mutilation/en/.

Contributor: Dan Kesselbrenner, National Immigration Project of the National Lawyers Guild.

---

[1] Congressional Research Service, *Asylum Law and Female Genital Mutilation: Recent Developments*, Feb. 15, 2008, http://fas.org/sgp/crs/misc/RS22810.pdf, (7/23/08).

[2] *Matter of A-T*, 24 I&N Dec. 296 (BIA 2007).

[3] INA §101(a)(42)(A), 8 U.S.C. §1101(a)(42)(A) (1982).

Bush "Law": State and Local Enforcement of Federal Immigration Law

Citation: The Illegal Immigration Reform and Immigrant Responsibility Act (IIRAIRA), 8 U.S.C. 1357.

Who is hurt by this "law": Unauthorized immigrants who live and work in communities that have §287g programs are subjected to racial profiling and reduced public safety. The law enforcement officers of states and localities that have §287g programs are now allowed to enforce federal immigration law, which means that they are able to ask about anyone's immigration status, whether the person they are asking has committed a crime or not.[1] If they determine that the person is illegally in the U.S. they can initiate deportation proceedings.[2] The law has been on the books for over a decade, but only during the Bush Administration has it actually been implemented. There are fifty-five active §287(g) programs and 80 pending requests. Immigration and Customs Enforcement (ICE) boasts that it has identified and imprisoned more than 60,000 people since January 2006.[3]

The §287g programs open the door for racial profiling because in their enforcement efforts, officers stop those who look foreign and patrol predominantly Latino neighborhoods in order to catch people for immigration violations. This provision and its enforcement, violate the decision of the U. S. Supreme Court in 1925[4] that deportation in not punishment, so deportees are not criminals and they are not entitled to the rights of those accused of committing crimes: right to counsel, trial by jury, proof beyond a reasonable doubt, etc. They are not to be arrested by law enforcement officers, federal or state, or detained in "prisons."[5]

In places where the IIRAIRA programs have been implemented, unauthorized immigrants are afraid to report crimes and injuries because they do not want the local police to come to their homes and question them about their immigration status.[6] These programs cultivate an atmosphere of fear because unauthorized immigrants are afraid to even go to the store for fear of being stopped by a police officer and questioned about their status.[7]

What the "law" provides: The Illegal Immigration Reform and Immigrant Responsibility Act (IIRAIRA) added §287(g) to the Immigration and Nationality Act. §287(g) authorizes the secretary of the Department of Homeland Security to enter into agreements ("Memorandum of Agreement" or MOA) with state and local law enforcement agencies, permitting officers to perform immigration law enforcement functions that historically have been reserved for federal law enforcement officers.[8]

What the "law" ignores:
   U.S. Constitution, General Welfare Clause, Art. 1, §8, cl. 2.
   U.S. Constitution, Fifth Amendment, Due Process Clause.
   U.S. Constitution, Privacy Right in Penumbra of First
      Amendment and Ninth Amendment.
   U.N. Charter, Preamble.
   U.N. Charter, Art. 55 & 56.
   ICCPR, Preamble.
   ICCPR, Art. 2(1).
   ICCPR, Art 17(1).
   ICCPR, Art. 23(1).
   ICCPR, Art. 26.
   ICAT, Art. 16(1).
   ICERD, Art. 2(1)(2).
   ICERD, Art. 5.

What Congress can do: In 2009, Congress can:

Repeal §287(g) of the INA and restore immigration enforcement exclusively to federal agents.

Remove immigration administrative warrants from the National Crime and Information Center Database.

---

[1] Deborah Jacobs and Ed Barocas, *AG's Guidance Needed on Cops and Immigrants, The Star-Ledger,* Jul. 27, 2007.

[2] Jennifer Ludden, *Local Police Taking On Immigration Enforcement, National Public Radio,* Jan. 11, 2008, http://www.npr.org/templates/story/story.php?storyId=18024294, (6/17/08).

[3] Id.

[4] *Bilokumsky v. Tod,* 263 U. S. 1479 (1923).

[5] People arrested by the Immigration and Naturalization Service were frequently housed in "separate quarters" that were, in fact, part of U. S. prisons.

[6] Supra note 1.

[7] Id.

[8] U.S. Immigration and Customs Enforcement, http://www.ice.gov/partners/287g/Section287_g.htm, (7/17/08).

LABOR

Bush "Law": Department of Labor and Office of Labor-Management Standards' Enforcement of Labor Management Reporting and Disclosure Act (Landrum-Griffin Act)

Citation: 29 U.S.C. §409, et seq.

Who is hurt by the improper enforcement of the "law": The Bush Administration has been heavily funding regulation of labor unions by the Department of Labor, while spending less money than in years past regulating the health and safety of workers, food quality, and air and water pollution.[1] Recently increased spending directed at the enforcement of reporting measures undermines labor unions' reputations.[2] Pres. Bush increased federal tax allocations for the Office of Labor Management Standards in order to "expand and exercise regulatory authority to impose costly and confusing new reporting requirements, attempt to increase the number of criminal prosecutions, [and] disclose the results to the public in seriously misleading ways..." according to the Center for American Progress.[3] The new emphasis on enforcement has increased the amount of paperwork for unions by an average of 60%, which, in turn, increases the amount of

100

time and expense involved and decreases the amount of money labor unions have for other union activities.[4] And the categories of spending that the Department of Labor now requires unions to report are not compatible with the categories that unions have in their budgets, so there is a second layer of accounting that is costly and confusing.[5] OLMS has misrepresented unions as increasingly corrupt by exaggerating the number of criminal actions by counting the conviction and sentencing of the same individual as two criminal actions rather than one.[6] The United Food and Commercial Workers (UCFW) is being hurt by enforcement of this law. Smithfield Co. sued alleging that UFCW was involved in the extortion and a pattern of racketeering activities under Racketeer Influenced and Corrupt Organizations Act (RICO).[7] In reality, UFCW was engaging in typical and lawful tactics used by unions to educate the public, pressure the employer corporation and gain public support. UFCW asked city councils to pass resolutions calling for the boycott of Smithfield products, demonstrated at stockholder meetings, filed complaints with OSHA. The judge ruled that the case should not be dismissed.[8]

What the "law" provides: The Landrum-Griffin Act governs labor unions and their organizations; its stated goal is to improve the governance of unions by preventing corruption and ensuring democratic governance.[9] Sec. 607 gives the Secretary of Labor the power to determine whether violations have occurred and the discretion as to whether to turn over facts to prosecutors.[10] The Bush Administration has allocated more money to the Office of Labor-Management Standards for enforcement and now requires disclosure of all receipts and expenditures by not only international labor unions, but all local unions and affiliates.[11]

What the "law" ignores:
U.S. Constitution, Fourteenth Amendment, Equal Protection Clause.
U.S. Constitution, General Welfare Clause, Art. I, §8, cl. 2.
U.S. Constitution, First Amendment.
International Covenant on Civil and Political Rights, Art. 22(1).

What Congress can do: In 2009, Congressmembers can not approve funding allocations that impose unnecessary paperwork on labor unions.[12]

[1] Scott Lilly, Center for American Progress, *Beyond Justice: Bush Administration's Labor Department Abuses Labor Union Regulatory Authorities*, December 2007, 1.

[2] Id. at 2.

[3] Id. at 2.

[4] Id. at 7, 8.

[5] Id. at 7.

[6] Id. at. 13.

[7] *Smithfield Foods, Inc. v. United Food & Commercial Workers Int'l Union et al.*, No. 3:07cv641 (E.D. Va. May 30, 2008).

[8] Jane Slaughter, *Corporate America Trying to Make Union Activities Illegal*, Mar. 26, 2008, http://www.alternet.org/rights/80464/, (7/15/08).

9 http://law.jrank.org/pages/8069/Landrum-Griffin-Act.html, (7/14/08).

[10] 29 U.S.C. 527, §607.

[11] Scott Lilly, Center for American Progress, *Beyond Justice: Bush Administration's Labor Department Abuses Labor Union Regulatory Authorities*, December 2007, 7.

Bush Policy and "Law": Exploitation of Low-wage Immigrant Workers and Proposed "No-Match" Regulations

Citation: Federal Register at Vol. 72, Number 157, p. 45615.

Who is hurt by this policy and "law": All low-wage immigrant workers, but especially those who are undocumented and working in low-wage jobs are hurt by exploitation. In 2005, there were an estimated 10 to 12 million undocumented immigrants in the U.S.[1], many of whom work in these low-wage, high-risk jobs, and there are several million more than that now. Foreign-born workers face a greater risk of death and injury than native-born workers, in part because foreign-born workers tend to work in high-risk industries, such as factory production lines and construction. Undocumented immigrant workers fear reporting injuries because they are largely unaware of their legal rights and their right to workers' compensation. Employers also intimidate workers into not reporting injuries and sometimes fire them when they get injured, citing immigration violations, to avoid paying workers' compensation.[2] "If an employer has no financial responsibility for work injuries for one class of workers, that creates a powerful perverse incentive for unscrupulous employers to hire that class of worker for the riskiest jobs," according to *Workers' Comp Insider*.[3]

Many of these problems will be exacerbated by Social Security "no-match" letters if the Department of Homeland Security's new regulations are implemented. Currently a judge has issued an injunction preventing implementation, but if the situation changes, it will not be good for immigrant workers.[4] This immigration enforcement tool will drive more workers into underground employment—which is not regulated at all—instead of its stated goal of reducing the employment of undocumented workers, according to the Immigrant and Nonstandard Worker Project.[5]

What the "law" provides: When employers hire new workers, they give the workers an I-9 form to fill out in order to verify their legal status. Workers fill out the form, including their name and social security number, and then these forms are sent to the Social Security Administration (SSA). If the name of the worker and the given social security number do not match, SSA sends a "no-match" letter to the employers telling them to take a number of steps to rectify the problem. Due to privacy rules, the SSA is not allowed to disclose the no-match information, but Immigration and Customs Enforcement (ICE) can require that employers turn over the no-match information. If these regulations go into effect, employers will likely just fire employees rather than go through the process to verify their employees' identification information.[6] In 2006, the Office of Inspector General reported that there are errors in the records of 17.8 million people, which means that these no-match letters may result in the firing of immigrant workers whose identification information is correct.[7]

What this policy and "law" ignore:

U.S. Constitution, General Welfare Clause, Art. I, §8, cl. 2.

U.N. Charter, Preamble.

U.N. Charter, Art. 55 & 56.

International Covenant on Civil and Political Rights (ICCPR), Preamble.

ICCPR, Art. 2(1).

ICCPR, Art. 5.

ICCPR, Art. 7: "No one shall be subjected to…cruel, inhuman or degrading treatment…"

ICCPR, Art. 26: "All persons are equal before the law and are entitled without any discrimination...on any ground such as race,... language,...national or social origin, birth..."
ICAT, Art. 16(1).

Bills proposed to improve conditions:

H.R. 4262: Safe, Orderly, Legal Visas and Enforcement Act of 2004 (introduced 5/4/04); sponsored by Rep. Luis Gutiérrez (D-IL) with 48 cosponsors.

S. 2381: Safe, Orderly, Legal Visas and Enforcement Act of 2004 (introduced 5/4/04); sponsored by Sen. Edward Kennedy (D-MA).

What Congress can do: In 2009, Congress can reintroduce and pass H.R. 4262/S. 2381 and pass additional legislation aimed at:

Better enforcement of antidiscrimination laws and enhanced public education;

More open vacancy notification systems for low-wage jobs;

Increasing enforcement of workplace standards including fair wage and overtime requirements, safety and health and labor laws; and

More job-skills training and adult education for all low-wage workers.

See also: AFL-CIO, Immigrant Workers, http//www.aficio.org/issues/civilrights/immigration/

Contributor: Dan Kesselbrenner, National Immigration Project of the National Lawyers Guild.

---

[1] Jeffery S. Passel, *Estimates of the Size and Characteristics of the Undocumented Population,* Washington D.C., Pew Hispanic Center, Mar. 21, 2005.

[2] Id.

[3] Julie Ferguson, *Injured Immigrant Workers Denied Workers' Compensation, Workers' Comp Insider,* Sept. 18, 2006, http://www.workerscompinsider.com/archives/000552.html, (7/22/08).

[4] http://aclu.org/immigrants/workplace/31537prs20070831.html (8/19/08).

[5] Immigrant and Nonstandard Worker Project, *Social Security No-Match Information and Employer Sanctions: Questions and Answers,* Nov. 2007, http://www.nelp.org/docUploads/SSA%5Fno%5Fmatch%5Fupdate%20110707%2Epdf, (7/22/08).

[6] Id at 6.

[7] Id. at 5-6.

Bush "Law": Lack of Enforcement of the Fair Labor Standards Act (FLSA)

Citation: 29 U.S.C. Ch. 8, 52 Stat. 1060, (1938).

Who is hurt by the lack of enforcement: Workers who have low-paying jobs are hurt by their employers' "wage-theft" and by the lack of enforcement of FLSA and the lack of investigations when workers report complaints to the Wage and Hour Division (WHD) of the Department of Labor (DoL).[1] Under the Bush Administration, the WHD closed at least 100 cases because of their inability to locate an employer and 350 cases were not assigned to an investigator until a year had passed since the complaint was filed.[2] The number of investigations by the WHD has fallen from 47,000 in 1997 to 30,000 in 2007.[3]

In July 2008, at a hearing before the House Education and Labor Committee, the Government Accountability Office (GAO) reported that the DoL mishandled overtime and minimum wage complaints and delayed the investigation of hundreds of cases for over a year. These complaints involved employers who were not paying their employees minimum wage, denying mandatory overtime pay, or not paying last paychecks. For example, an employer did not give a truck driver overtime pay, despite the fact that the truck driver worked 55 hours a week. The WHD did not investigate until 17 months after the complaint was made and then dropped the case six months later because the statute of limitations was nearing.[4] The WHD dropped another case involving the use of disabled children to operate heavy machinery, which violates child-labor laws, because the WHD investigators could not find the employer.[5]

What the law provides: The Fair Labor Standards Act was passed in 1938 and addresses federal labor issues. Sec. 206 of the Act governs the federal minimum wage. Sec. 207 establishes time-and-a-half pay for overtime work. Sec. 212 prohibits "oppressive child labor." The WHD is responsible for enforcing federal labor laws including those on minimum wage, overtime pay, family and medical leave, migrant workers, recordkeeping, and others.[6]

What law the lack of enforcement ignores:
Fair Labor Standards Act.
U.S. Constitution, General Welfare Clause, Art. I, §8, cl. 1.
U.S. Constitution, Fifth Amendment, Due Process Clause.

U.N. Charter, Art. 55 & 56.

International Covenant on Civil and Political Rights (ICCPR), Preamble.

ICCPR, Art. 1(1): "All people have the right of self-determination.By virtue of that right they...freely pursue their economic, social and cultural development."

ICCPR, Art. 1(2): "...In no case may a people be deprived of its own means of subsistence."

ICCPR, Art. 2(1).

ICERD, Art. 2(2), 5(e), (i), (ii), (iv).

What Congress can do: In 2009, Congressmembers can pass legislation to increase enforcement of the FLSA through more specific funding for that purpose.

See also: Full Committee Hearing: "Is the Department of Labor Effectively Enforcing Our Wage and Hour Laws?" July, 15, 2008. Available at: http://edlabor.house.gov/hearings/fc-2008-07-15.shtml.

---

[1] Testimony of Kim Bobo, Executive Director of Interfaith Worker Justice before the Committee on Education and Labor, U.S. House of Representatives at the hearing on "Is the Department of Labor Effectively Enforcing Our Wage and Hour Laws?", July 15, 2008.

[2] Stephen Greenhouse, *Department is Criticized on Disputes Over Wages, New York Times,* July 15, 2008.

[3] Mike Hall, *Employer Doesn't Pay You? Under Bush Wage and Hour Dept., You're Out of Luck, AFL-CIO NOW Blog,* July 16, 2008, http://blog.aflcio.org/2008/07/16/employer-doesnt-pay-you-under-bush-wage-and-hour-dept-youre-out-of-luck/, (7/29/08).

[4] Id.

[5] Editorial, *No Friend of the Workers, New York Times*, July 18, 2008.

[6] U.S. Department of Labor: Employment Standards Division, Wage and Hour Division, http://www.dol.gov/esa/whd/, (7/29/08)

MILITARY COMMISSIONS

Bush Law: Military Commissions Act of 2006 (MCA) – Suspension of Habeas Corpus as to Alien Detainees

See also: Detention, supra.

Citation: Public Law 109-336, 120 Stat. 2616 (2006).

Who is hurt by this law: After the terrorist attacks of 9/11, Bush asked and Congress passed the Authorization for Use of Military Force (Pub. L. 107-40, §2(a), Sept. 18, 2001) and cites it as justification for widespread arrests of at least 775 individuals worldwide[1] and their indefinite detention at Guantanamo Bay in Cuba, Abu Ghraib in Iraq, and elsewhere. Of these, after years in detention, at least 40 attempted suicide,[2] three succeeded in committing suicide,[3] and at least 128 others went on hunger strike only to have U.S. soldiers force feed them. The U.S. still holds 270 detainees at Guantanamo Bay Naval Base in Cuba.[4]

What the law provides: In 2006, at Bush's request, Congress passed the Military Commissions Act (MCA) stripping federal courts of jurisdiction to hear habeas corpus petitions by alien detainees. MCA Sec. 7(a) "...No court, justice, or judge shall have jurisdiction to hear or consider an application for a writ of habeas corpus filed by or on behalf of an alien detainee by the United States who has been determined by the United States to have been properly detained as an enemy combatant or is awaiting such determination." This section was struck down June 12, 2008 by the U.S. Supreme Court in *Boumediene v. Bush.*[5]

What the law ignores:

U.S. Constitution Art. I, Sec. 2, Cl. 2: "The privilege of the Writ of Habeas Corpus shall not be suspended, unless when in Cases of Rebellion or Invasion the public Safety may require it."

U.S. Constitution, Fifth Amendment, Due Process Clause.

U.N. Charter, Preamble.

U.N. Charter, Art. 55 & 56.

ICCPR, Preamble.

ICCPR, Art. 9(1): "Everyone has the right to liberty and security of person. No one shall be subjected to arbitrary arrest or detention. No one shall be deprived of his liberty except on such grounds and in accordance with such procedure as are established by law."

ICCPR, Art. 9(2): "Anyone who is arrested shall be informed, at the time of arrest, of reasons of his arrest and shall be promptly informed of any charges against him."

ICCPR, Art. 9(4): "Anyone who is deprived of his liberty by arrest or detention shall be entitled to proceedings before a court, in order that the court may decide without delay on the lawfulness of his detention and order his release if the detention is not lawful."

ICCPR, Art. 10(1).

ICERD, Art. 5.

Bills introduced to undo the law:

S.576: Restoring the Constitution Act of 2007, (introduced 2/13/07); sponsored by Sen. Christopher Dodd (D-CT) with 13 cosponsors.

H.R. 1415: Restoring the Constitution Act of 2007, (introduced 3/8/07); sponsored by Rep. Jerrold Nadler (D-NY) with 76 cosponsors.

S.185: Habeas Corpus Restoration Act of 2007, (introduced 1/4/07); sponsored by Sen. Arlen Specter (R-PA) with 31 cosponsors.

H.R. 1416: Habeas Corpus Restoration Act of 2007, (introduced 3/8/07); sponsored by Rep. Jerrold Nadler (D-NY) with 86 cosponsors.

What Congress can do: In 2009, Congress members can refuse to approve any law that eliminates habeas corpus. The House Judiciary Committee and the Senate Committee can hold hearings and call government witnesses to ask whether this Supreme Court decision is being enforced.

See also: http://www.aclu.org/safefree/detention/commissions.html

108

[1] www.defenselink.mil, News Releases, Dec. 20, 2007, (5/27/08).

[2] Carol J. Williams, LA Times, May 19, 2006.

[3] Carol D. Leonnig, Washington Post, Sept. 13, 2005.

[4] www.defenselink.mil, News Releases, May 2, 2008, (5/7/08).

[5] *Boumedine v. Bush*, 553 U.S. (Decided June 12, 2008), Docket # 06-1195.

MILITARY RECRUITMENT

Bush "Law": Expedited Naturalization Executive Order, and National Defense Authorization Act of 2006

Citation: Exec. Order No. 13,269 (July 3, 2002) and Public Law 109-163, 119 Stat. 3136.

Who is hurt by this "law": Both legal immigrants and undocumented immigrants are being recruited by the U.S. military because it has been having trouble recruiting new soldiers; 2005 had the lowest recruitment numbers for the Army in years.[1] The military has been recruiting using Spanish-language radio ads, offering English language classes, and promising citizenship to enlistees.[2] Undocumented families in the U.S. are returning home because they fear their children will be recruited to go to war.[3] The Department of Defense maintains it does not recruit unauthorized immigrants but military recruiters are still targeting the undocumented by offering them and their families green cards, even though everyone must go through the legalization process individually.[4] The military itself has no power to grant citizenship; this process is conducted through U. S. Citizenship and Immigration Services (USCIS). The *Boston Globe* reports that "officials have also raised concerns that immigrants would be disproportionately sent to the front lines as 'cannon fodder' in any conflict".[5] The Pew Hispanic Center Study found Latinos are "underrepresented in some of the more technical occupations such as electronics and communication," over represented among enlisted personnel who "most directly handle weapons."[6]

What the "law" provides: Pres. Bush issued the Expedited Naturalization Executive Order on July 3, 2002 that provided for the "expedited naturalization for aliens and noncitizen nationals serving in an active-duty status in the Armed Forces...during the period of war against terrorists of global reach."[7] The National

Defense Authorization Act of 2006 codified this Executive Order that purportedly only applies to noncitizens that are lawfully in the country. The Development, Relief, and Education for Alien Minors Act (DREAM Act, S. 2205) would offer a path to citizenship to unauthorized immigrants if they complete two years of college or two years of military service.

What the "law" ignores:

U.S. Constitution, General Welfare Clause, Art. I, §8, cl. 1.
U.N. Charter, Art. 2(4).
ICCPR, Art. 26.
ICERD, Art. I, §1-4.
ICERD, Art. II, § 1-2.
ICERD, Art. VII.

What Congress can do: In 2009, Congress can: (1) hold hearings on alleged targeting of Spanish-speaking youth; (2) pass a resolution forbidding sending immigrants to the front lines in Iraq or Afghanistan disproportionately; (3) reject any new DREAM Act.

See also: D.C. Anti-War Network, http://www.counter-recruitment.org

---

[1] *Army's Recruiting Lowest in Years, Associated Press*, September

[2] Summer Harlow, *Military recruiters set sights on Hispanics, The News Journal*, August 20, 2007.

[3] Press TV, *U.S. Military Recruiting Illegal Aliens*, December, 2007, http://www.presstv.ir/detail.aspx?id=36682&sectionid=3510203, (6/8/08).

[4] Deborah Davis, *Yo Soy el Army, Metroactive*, September 17, 2007, http://www.metroactive.com/metro/09.19.07/news-0738.html, (6/8/08).

[5] Bryan Bender, *Military Considers Recruiting Foreigners, The Boston Globe,* December 26, 2006.

[6] Pew Hispanic Center, *Hispanics in the Military,* March 27, 2003.

[7] Exec. Order 13,269 (July 3, 2002).

Bush Law: No Child Left Behind Act of 2001 (NCLB)

Citation: Public Law 107-110, 20 U.S.C. §7908.

Who is hurt by this law: In the 1980s, some states required school districts to give lists of their graduating seniors to recruiters.[1] Now, the No Child Left Behind Act requires *all*

public schools to give lists *and contact information* of *all* of their students.[2] Children as young as eleven are being approached and influenced by military recruiters at school through "heavy-handed recruitment tactics and misconduct by recruiters".[3] The Women's International League for Peace and Freedom (WILPF) submitted a statement to the U. N. Committee on the Rights of the Child (CRC) regarding U.S. compliance with the CRC's Optional Protocol on Children in Armed Conflict, which the U.S. has both signed and ratified. In this statement, WILPF claims that U.S. military recruiters are violating the minimum safeguards required by the Optional Protocol.[4] In 2005, seventeen year olds made up 4.5% of new active recruits to the armed forces and 15% of all new recruits to the reserves.[5] Schools in low-income neighborhoods often rely on military funded programs, like JROTC, so their other programs can 'make financial ends meet.'[6]

What the law provides:

§9528(a)(1): "...each local educational agency receiving assistance under this Act shall provide, on a request made by military recruiters...access to secondary school students names, addresses, and telephone listings."

The only way for parents or students to withhold their personal information is through an opt-out provision, so if parents and students are unaware of this provision (§9228(a)(2)), their personal information will be given to recruiters.

What the law ignores:

Optional Protocol on Children in Armed Conflict (CRC OPAC), Art. 3(3): "States Parties that permit voluntary recruitment into their national armed forces under the age of 18...shall maintain safeguards to ensure,...that: (a) Such recruitment is genuinely voluntary; (b)...is carried out with the informed consent of the person's parents or legal guardians; (c) Such persons are fully informed of the duties involved in such military service;..."

U.S. Constitution, General Welfare Clause, Art. I, §8, cl. 1.

The privacy protections in the penumbra of the First and Ninth Amendments.

U. N. Charter, Art. 55 (c).

ICCPR, Art. 2(1).

ICCPR, Art. 17(1).

ICCPR, Art. 24(1).

What Congress can do: In 2009, Congressmembers can repeal the entire No Child Left Behind Act or the military recruitment provision (20 U.S.C. §1708).

And see: "Racial Disparities in Education and Opportunities in the United States, Violations of the International Convention on Elimination of Racial Discrimination: A Response to the 2007 Report of the U.S.", by Lawyers' Comm. for Civil Rights Under Law, Center for Human Rights and Humanitarian Law, Leitner Center for Int'l Law & Justice, Jewish Council on Urban Affairs, Mexican American Legal Defense & Educ. Fund, Nat'l. Economic & Social Rights Initiative, NAACP Legal Defense & Educational Fund, Inc., NYU School of Law, Poverty & Race Research Action Council, The Advocates for Human Rights, U of Pa. Law School, Human Rights Advocates and Frank C. Newman International Human Rights Clinic, Urban Justice Center in *Seattle Journal for Social Justice,* Vol. 6 issue 2, pp. 591-647.

See also: Women's International League for Peace & Freedom (WILPF), http://wilpf.org/files/WILPFStatementToCRC_ReOPAC_Feb2008.pdf

---

[1] Rev. Daniel Buford, *Marketing the Military: Should Soldiering Be Sold Like Soap?, Media & Values #39,* 1987.

[2] No Child Left Behind Act of 2001, 20 U.S.C. §7908.

[3] American Civil Liberties Union, *Soldiers of Misfortune: Abusive U.S. Military Recruitment and Failure to Protect Child Soldiers,* May 2008.

[4] Women's International League for Peace and Freedom, *Statement to the Committee on the Rights of the Child regarding U.S. Compliance with CRC OPAC,* February 7, 2008.

[5] Id.

[6] Id.

NATIVE AMERICAN/TRIBAL LAND AND RIGHTS

Bush Law: Western Shoshone Claims Distribution Act of 2004

Citation: Public Law 108-270.

Who is hurt by this law: The Timbisha Shoshone Tribe, the Yomba Shoshone Tribe, the Wells Band of Western Shoshone, and the Te-Moak Tribe of Western Shoshone are hurt by this law permitting U.S. government agencies to invade their ancestral territory that encompasses 60 million acres stretching from southern Idaho, western Utah, across Nevada, and down to the Mojave Desert of California, the third largest gold producing area in the world cited by a 1999 Department of Interior report as the number one investment opportunity for extraction companies.[1]

The mining of Tribal lands will mean higher levels of mercury emissions and greater exposure to toxic contamination for people who already live in Nevada, the state with the highest levels of mercury pollution in the U.S.[2]

Nuclear testing will have an environmental impact on Yucca Mountain, long a place of powerful spiritual energy for the Shoshone and the Paiute.[3] Bush has designated Yucca Mountain as the nation's nuclear waste repository and the home to the Nevada Test Site (NTS) and Federal Counterterrorism Facility.[4] All living things are at risk in this dynamic desert bioregion with hundreds of plant, animal and bird species that freely cross NTS boundaries and interbreed well beyond NTS borders. Some species continue to be harvested by humans for food and medicinal uses, and therefore have potential contaminant-carrier impacts.[5]

Surface and ground water: In addition to being carried on the wind in many directions, particulate matter is commonly

114

transported in colloidal or other forms through surface and groundwater, and all water paths lead off the Test Site to the Amargosa Desert in Nevada and California. Plutonium 239 is of particular concern, for thousands of years to come.[6] The other sites are: Kansas City Plant, Kansas City, Missouri; Lawrence Livermore National Laboratory, Livermore, California; Los Alamos, Santa Fe, New Mexico; Savannah River Site, Aiken, South Carolina; Pantex Plant, Amarillo, Texas; Y-12 National Security Complex, Oakridge, Tennessee; Sandia National Laboratories in Albuquerque, New Mexico; Livermore, California, and Tonopah, Nevada.[7]

What the law provides:

In July 2004, Bush signed the law that allows Western Shoshone tribal members to each receive $15,000 to $30,000 for their land, forcibly distributing 24 million acres of land in Nevada, Utah, California and Idaho, based on the Ruby Valley Treaty of 1863, through payment by the U.S. government based on an 1872 price, roughly 15 cents an acre.[8] The National Park Service, U.S. Fish and Wildlife Service, Bureau of Land Management and Bureau of Indian Affairs have all signed on to the agreement with the Southern Nevada Water Authority ("SNWA").[9] Yucca Mountain is one of eight locations considering establishment of a consolidated plutonium center and a special nuclear material consolidation site under the Complex Transformation.[10]

What the law ignores:

The original U.S. Department of the Interior opposition to the water diversion plan.[11]

The protests of the Western Shoshone.

Treaty of Ruby Valley with the Western Shoshone Nation in 1863.[12]

U.S. Constitution, Art. 6, cl. 2.

ICCPR, Preamble.

ICCPR, Art. 27: "In those States in which ethnic, ...minorities exist, persons belonging to such minorities shall not be denied the right, in community with the other members of their group, to enjoy their own culture, ..."

ICERD, Art. 5.

ICERD Concluding Observation, February 2008, #19.[13]

ICERD Concluding Observation, February 2008, #29.[14]

Bill Proposed To Stop the Shoshone Claims Distribution Act: H.R. 2262: Hardrock Mining and Reclamation Act of 2007: Allows states or Indian tribes to petition the Secretary of the Interior to withdraw tracts of Federal land from the operation of mining laws in order to protect values such as watersheds that supply drinking water, wildlife habitat, cultural or historic resources, or scenic vistas important to the local economy (Sec. 202). (introduced 5/10/07); sponsored by Rep. Nick Rahall (D-WV) with 62 cosponsors.

What Congress Can Do: In 2009, Congress can: (1) repeal the Complex Transformation project under the National Defense Authorization Act for Fiscal Year 2008; (2) pass HR. 2262: Hardrock Mining and Reclamation Act of 2007.

---

[1] Posted: July 7, 2004, by: Western Shoshone Defense Project
http://www.h-o-m-e.org/Shoshone/Shoshone%20Docs/Distribution.Dann.htm

[2] Great Basin Mine Watch, et al, "Glamis Gold Caught Under-Reporting Mercury Releases" Press Release (Nov. 15, 2006) (App. 8).

[3] http://www.sacredland.org/endangered_sites_pages/yucca_mountain.html

[4] http://www.h-o-m-e.org/Shoshone/Shoshone%20Docs/Distribution.Dann.htm

[5] Western Shoshone National Council, Update to Early Warning and Urgent Action Procedure Decision 1(68), February 7, 2007.

[6] http://www.h-o-m-e.org/Weapons/DS%20comments2-7-07.pdf Comments on the DRAFT December 2006 Revised Environmental Assessment (EA) on Large-Scale, Open-Air Explosive Detonation DIVINE STRAKE at the Nevada Test Site.

[7] http://nnsa.energy.gov/defense_programs/complex_transformation.htm

[8] Posted: July 09, 2004, by: Jerry Reynolds / Washington D.C. correspondent / Indian Country Today http://www.indiancountry.com/?1089383970

[9] Henry Brean, "$2 Billion Project: Water Authority Gets Deal: Federal Agency Ends Protest of Plan to Tap Rural County," Las Vegas Journal (Sept. 12, 2006) (App. 13). http://www.reviewjournal.com/lvrj_home/2006/Sep-12-Tue-2006/news/9600067.html

[10] See Complex Transformation under "National Defense Authorization Act for Fiscal Year 2008".

[11] Brean, supra note 9.

[12] http://www.nativeweb.org/pages/legal/shoshone/ruby_valley.html

[13] "While noting the explanations provided by the State party with regard

to the situation of the Western Shoshone indigenous peoples, considered by the Committee under its early warning and urgent action procedure, the Committee strongly regrets that the State party has not followed up on the recommendations contained in paragraphs 8 to 10 of its decision 1(68) of 2006 (ICERD/C/USA/DEC/1). (Article 5) The Committee reiterates its Decision 1 (68) in its entirety, and urges the State party to implement all the recommendations contained therein."

[14] "The Committee is concerned about reports relating to activities – such as nuclear testing, toxic and dangerous waste storage, mining or logging – carried out or planned in areas of spiritual and cultural significance to Native Americans, and about the negative impact that such activities allegedly have on the enjoyment by the affected indigenous peoples of their rights under the Convention. (Articles 5 (d) (v), 5 (e) (iv) and 5 (e) (vi)) The Committee recommends that the State party take all appropriate measures – in consultation with indigenous peoples concerned and their representatives chosen in accordance with their own procedures – to ensure that activities carried out in areas of spiritual and cultural significance to Native Americans do not have a negative impact on the enjoyment of their rights under the Convention. The Committee further recommends that the State party recognise the right of Native Americans to participate in decisions affecting them, and consult and cooperate in good faith with the indigenous peoples concerned before adopting and implementing any activity in areas of spiritual and cultural significance to Native Americans. While noting the position of the State party with regard to the United Nations Declaration on the Rights of Indigenous Peoples (A/RES/61/295), the Committee finally recommends that the declaration be used as a guide to interpret the State party's obligations under the Convention relating to indigenous peoples."

PRISON ADMINISTRATION

Bush Law: Prison Rape Elimination Act of 2003

Citation: 42 U.S.C. 15601.

Who is hurt by this law: The U. S. prison population reached 2,299,116 in 2001.[1] Many of these prisoners are poor people, disproportionately African Americans and Latinos. The resulting overcrowding of our nation's prisons, inadequate healthcare for prisoners, the prevalence of infectious diseases, and increased violence and abuse of prisoners have an impact on our whole society. Our whole society is also hurt when a U. S. government body fails to make changes set forth in a report by the Office of Inspector General, as in the OIG Report of 2005.[2] Over the course of a year, 13.5 million people spend time in jail or prison, and 95 percent of them eventually return to our communities.[3]

What the law provides: In 2003, Bush signed the Prison Rape Elimination Act (PREA) to provide annual appropriations of $60 million for each fiscal year from 2004 through 2010.[4] The National Prison Rape Elimination Commission (NPREC) was created to study and develop national zero tolerance standards for the prevention of and response to sexual abuse in all confinement settings including lockups, small and large jails, state and federal prisons, juvenile facilities, immigration detention facilities, and community corrections facilities. These standards relate to training, inmate classification, reporting of incidents, investigation and resolution of complaints, preservation of evidence, medical and mental health care for victims, and data collection.

No more than 2 years after the initial meeting of the NPREC they were to submit their final report.[5] Within a year of receiving the Commission's final report, the Attorney General is required by the statute to consider the Commission's recommended standards and to promulgate national standards for the detection, prevention, reduction, and punishment of prison rape. Those standards will apply to the Federal Bureau of Prisons immediately on adoption. States will receive notification of the new standards from the U.S. Attorney General, and will have a year to adopt and comply with them or risk losing 5% of any federal grants for prison purposes.[6]

After five years, NPREC has not produced a completed study report after announcing it would be submitted to Congress in July 2007.[7] NPREC[8] is now scheduled to impose substantial additional costs compared to the costs presently expended by Federal, State and local prison authorities.[9] "The second deficiency is that they do not apply when federal inmates are held in facilities under contract to the federal government rather than in BOP facilities."[10]

What the law ignores:
U.S. Constitution, Eighth Amendment.
Prison Litigation Reform Act of 1996.[11]
U.N. Charter, Preamble, Art. 1.
ICAT, Preamble, Art. 1, 2, 4, 5-7, 9-14, 16.
ICCPR, Preamble, Art. 2-5, 7, 10, 16, 17, 26.
ICERD, Preamble, Art. 1, 2, 4, 5 (a)(b)(e)(iv), 6, and 7.

What Congress can do: In 2009, Congress can impose higher sentencing guidelines for staff sexual abuse of inmates according to the 2005 OIG report[12] and pass the following bills:

H.R.4109: Prison Abuse Remedies Act of 2007: Amends the Civil Rights of Institutionalized Persons Act to: (1) eliminate the requirement of a prior showing of physical injury before a prisoner may bring a claim for mental or emotional injury while in custody; and (2) provide for a 90-day stay of nonfrivolous claims regarding prison conditions to allow prison officials to consider such claims through the administrative process; (3) exclude from the application of such Act prisoners under the age of 18; and (4) eliminate certain restrictions on awarding attorney fees in civil actions brought by prisoners. (introduced 11/07/07; sponsored by Rep. Robert Scott (D-VA) with 9 cosponsors).

H.R.1889: Private Prison Information Act of 2007: Provides that each nongovernmental entity contracting with the federal government to incarcerate and/or detain federal prisoners in a privately-owned facility shall have the same duty to release information about the operation of that facility as a federal agency would have under the Freedom of Information Act. Authorizes any aggrieved party to obtain relief in a civil action. (introduced 4/17/07; sponsored by Rep. Tim Holden (D-PA) with 24 cosponsors).

S. 2010: (identical to H.R. 1889) (introduced 8/3/07; sponsored by Sen. Joe Lieberman (I-CT) with 2 cosponsors).

See also: http://www.prisoncommission.org/

---

[1] http://www.ojp.usdoj.gov/bjs/prisons.htm

[2] http://www.usdoj.gov/oig/special/0504/index.htm

[3] http://www.prisoncommission.org/report.asp

[4] Pat Kaufman. "Prison Rape: Research Explores Prevalence, Prevention." National Institute of Justice Journal, Issue No. 259, April 2008.

[5] http://www.nprec.us/docs/Prison_Rape_Elimination_Act_of_2003.pdf

[6] http://www.nprec.us/UpcomingEvents/NPREC_StandardsProcess.May2008.pdf

[7] NPREC letter to Congress dated 7/21/2006.

[8] http://www.spr.org/en/programs.asp

[9] Public Law 108-79, Prison Rape Elimination Act of 2003, (117 Stat. 984).

[10] http://www.usdoj.gov/oig/special/0504/index.htm

[11] "Intended to limit the number of frivolous lawsuits filed by inmates, the PLRA has instead greatly undermined the crucial oversight role played by courts in addressing sexual assault and other constitutional violations in corrections facilities." http://www.spr.org/pdf/PREA_Update_June_2008.pdf

12 Supra, note 2.

TAXES

Bush Law: Economic Growth and Tax Reconciliation Act of 2001

Citation: Public Law 107-16 (2001).

Who has been hurt by this law: The tax cuts in 2001—and the subsequent cuts throughout the Bush Administration—will result in a total loss of federal revenue of almost $1,800,000,000,000 by the time they expire in 2010.[1] This law cuts income taxes and estate taxes, but not payroll taxes, so it does relatively little to provide tax breaks for the poorer half of the U.S. The U.S. has a total national debt of $9,400,000,000,000 as of June 2008.[2] Low- and middle-income families may have to pay the bill for these tax cuts on higher incomes, so they would have been better off if this law had never been enacted. These tax cuts have been deficit-financed, meaning the U.S. has had to borrow to make up the lost revenue. The resulting debt – plus interest – must be paid off. The danger: that the middle-class will end up paying the bill through cuts in public services or future tax increases. Pres. Bush has continued to propose budget cuts that affect programs such as the Perkins loan program, which provides loans to lower-income college students, as well as loan forgiveness for Armed Service members and Peace Corps volunteers.[3] In 2006, the budget cuts reduced the Department of Agriculture's funding by $2,000,000,000, taking away funds from rural development, research, watershed protection, and

121

renewable energy.[4] That year, Bush requested that $500,000,000 be cut from the Environmental Protection Agency's budget, which affected land preservation, water quality protection programs, and loans for states to build sewage and water treatment plants.[5] Budget cuts in 2006 also targeted hospitals by reducing health care spending on Medicare and Medicaid by $196,000,000,000 over the next five years.[6]

These budget cuts also: (1) mean that, overall, government agencies have less money to spend on services for low- and middle-income families needing public service -- health care, education, and transportation; (2) these agencies then cannot make plans to expand their most successful programs because they cannot rely on future funding.

Officially, the 2001 tax legislation was estimated to reduce federal revenues by $1,350,000,000,000 over 10 years, plus associated added interest on the national debt. The true, much higher cost was masked by phasing in many of the tax cuts over several years.

What the law provides: At Pres. Bush's request, Congressmembers passed the Act of 2001, which amended the U.S. Internal Revenue Code to phase in various income tax, estate tax, and gift tax cuts over 9 years. Under the plan, the poorest 78 million people save an annual average of only $347, while the richest 1.3 million save an average of $53,120.[7] Median income taxpayers have seen only a $600 tax cut.[8]

The following cuts were made in the income tax rates for each bracket, from highest to lowest:

39.6% to 35%
6% to 33%
31% to 28%
28% to 25%

The 15% rate was left in place, but many people formerly subject to that rate are now in the new 10% bracket created by this law.

The law includes an expansion in the child tax credit and the earned income tax credit, both of which help poor and middle-class families, but these changes are small compared to the cuts in the income tax and the estate tax.

122

The estate tax was scheduled to shrink each year until disappearing altogether in 2010.

Several changes were made to increase the tax subsidies for certain retirement and education savings, which probably do little to encourage saving but benefit well-off families for making savings they would have made anyway.

These provisions, along with almost all Bush tax cuts, will expire at the end of 2010.

What the law ignores:

U.S. Constitution, General Welfare Clause, Art. I, §8, cl. 1.
U.N. Charter, Art. 55 & 56.
ICCPR, Art. 1, §1.
ICCPR, Art. 1, §2.
ICCPR, Art. 2, § 1.
ICERD, Art I, §1.
ICERD, Art. II, §1c, §2.
ICERD, Art. V, (d)(v), (e)(iv)(v).
ICERD, Art. 6.
ICERD, Art. 7.

What Congress can do: In 2009, Congressmembers can either:

Repeal the Economic Growth and Tax Reconciliation Act;
Repeal the Bush income tax cuts for taxpayers in the top three income tax brackets;
Repeal the cuts in the estate tax;
Repeal the tax cuts for retirement savings;
Propose legislation to restore taxes.

See also: Citizens for Tax Justice, www.ctj.org

---

[1] Brookings Institution, http://www.brookings.edu/articles/2004/0919useconomics_gale.aspx, (6/24/08).

[2] U.S. Department of Treasury, http://www.treasurydirect.gov/NP/BPDLogin?application=np, (6/24/08).

[3] Michael Fletcher, *2006 Budget Proposal: Agency Breakdown, Washington Post,* 2/7/05, http://www.washingtonpost.com/wp-srv/politics/interactives/budget06/budget06Agencies.html, (6/25/08).

[4] Dan Morgan, *2006 Budget Proposal: Agency Breakdown, Washington Post,* 2/7/05, http://www.washingtonpost.com/wp-srv/politics/

interactives/budget06/budget06Agencies.html, (6/25/08).

5 Shankar Vedantam, *2006 Budget Proposal: Agency Breakdown*, *Washington Post*, 2/7/05, http://www.washingtonpost.com/wp-srv/politics/interactives/budget06/budget06Agencies.html, (6/25/08).

6 Doug Trapp, *Bush Budget Cuts Hospital Funding But Silent on Medicare Doctor Pay*, AMNews, 2/18/07, http://www.ama-assn.org/amednews/2008/02/18/gvl10218.htm, (6/24/08).

7 Citizens for Tax Justice, http://www.ctj.org/html/gwbfinal.htm, (6/24/08).

8 Citizens for Tax Justice, http://www.ctj.org/html/gwbfinal.htm, (6/24/08).

Bush Law: The Jobs and Growth Reconciliation Tax Act of 2003

Citation: Public Law 108-27, 117 Stat. 752.

Who is hurt by this law: A middle-manager in a factory may pay taxes at a higher rate than a billionaire heir whose wealth comes from stock. The federal treasury suffers because the wealthy use investment accounting methods to turn their income into capital gains taxed at the lower rate. Most stock owned by middle-income people is in 401(k) plans, Individual Retirement Accounts (IRAs) or other retirement savings vehicles. Taxes on these are deferred until retirement, then they are taxed as "ordinary income"--they don't benefit from the tax cuts for capital gains and dividends, and will lose when the federal deficit must be paid off.To pay this off, about one and a half trillion dollars have been added to the national debt during the Bush years, due to Bush tax cuts. Congress will have to increase taxes, cut back public services that residents depend on, or both.

What the law provides: In 2001, dividends were taxed as ordinary income (for the wealthiest this meant a top marginal rate of 39.6 percent). The top rate for capital gains had recently been lowered from 28 percent to 20 percent. In 2003, Pres. Bush got Congress to lower the top rate for both capital gains and corporate stock dividends to 15 percent.

The 2003 Tax Cut Act extended some corporate loopholes, slashed taxes for investment income (capital gains and dividends), and accelerated the phasing in of some of the tax cuts already enacted in 2001.

124

Citizens for Tax Justice has calculated that in 2009, 70 percent of the benefits of the capital gains and dividends tax cuts will go to the richest one percent of U.S. residents.

What the law ignores:

U.S. Constitution, General Welfare Clause, Art. I,§ 8, cl. 2.

U.N. Charter, Art. 55 and 56.

International Covenant on Civil and Political Rights (ICCPR), Art. 2, § 1: "Each State Party...undertakes...to ensure to all individuals...subject to its jurisdiction the rights recognized in the present Covenant, without distinction...such as race...social origin, property,...or other status."

ICCPR, Art. 1, § 1: "All peoples have the right to...freely determine their political status and freely pursue their economic, social and cultural development."

Bills proposed to undo the 2003 Bush tax cuts:

Sen. Barack Obama (D-IL) has proposed repealing the Bush tax cuts for families with incomes over $250,000; to tax their dividends as ordinary income and repeal the capital gains tax cut if elected President he said he might propose raising the highest tax rate for capital gains to around 25 percent.

What Congress can do: The 2009 Congress can tax income from investments just like income from work: both capital gains and dividends can be taxed as ordinary income.

Submitted by: Steve Wamhoff, Legislative Director, Citizens for Tax Justice, www.ctj.org

Bush Law: The American Jobs Creation Act of 2004

Citation: Public Law 108-357.

Who is hurt by this law: The 2004 tax cut bill brought U. S. further down the path of freeing businesses from their tax obligations and shifting the responsibility for supporting public services to low- and middle-income U. S. taxpayers. The law made the tax code much more complex, creating new tax loopholes for businesses. The law creates more loopholes in the tax code that lead investors to make investments based on tax considerations rather than the type that are likely to create more jobs and grow the economy the most.

What the law provides: This law began just before the 2004 election as an attempt to resolve a trade dispute between the U. S. and Europe over a $5 billion a year U.S. tax subsidy for U.S. exporters that had been (repeatedly) ruled illegal by the World Trade Organization. It expanded into corporate tax giveaways totaling $214 billion over five years.

The small and relatively unknown tax subsidy that was declared illegal was replaced by a larger and more complicated tax subsidy: the deduction for domestic production. Another provision -- the new "worldwide interest allocation" rules -- is designed to make it easier for multinational corporations to take U.S. tax deductions for interest payments that are really expenses of earning foreign profits and therefore should not be deductible. The law also made it easier for companies to use credits against their U.S. taxes for taxes paid to foreign governments and included a variety of other tax changes that opponents say were passed to gain campaign contributions in 2004.

The law was said by its proponents to be revenue-neutral, but critics claim that rested on a series of accounting gimmicks. E.g. some provisions were scheduled to fully take effect only at the end of the period of years considered by the budget procedures, and some provisions were made "temporary" even though proponents knew full well that they intended to extend these provisions indefinitely.

What the law ignores:

U.S. Constitution, General Welfare Clause, Art. I,§ 8, cl. 2.

U.N. Charter, Art. 55 and 56.

International Covenant on Civil and Political Rights (ICCPR), Art. 2, § 1: "Each State Party...undertakes...to ensure to all individuals...subject to its jurisdiction the rights recognized in the present Covenant, without distinction...such as race...social origin, property,...or other status."

ICCPR, Art. 1, § 1: "All peoples have the right to...freely determine their political status and freely pursue their economic, social and cultural development."

Bills proposed to undo the 2004 Bush tax cuts:

By Aug. 1, 2008, Presidential candidate Sen. Barack Obama had proposed repealing tax loopholes that encourage the movement of business investment offshore, but had not called for repealing any specific provisions of this law. The campaign staff of Sen. John McCain said that he would repeal the domestic production deduction.

What Congress can do: In 2009, Congress can repeal most of the new tax cuts created in the 2004 law.

See also: Citizens for Tax Justice, www.ctj.org

Bush Law: Internet Tax Freedom Act Amendments Act of 2007

Citation: Public Law 110-108.

Who is hurt by this law: States with sales taxes that are not allowed to levy taxes on commercial internet transactions are hurt by the loss of revenue that such taxes would generate. There is no federal sales tax in the U.S. and states are responsible for deciding whether they want to levy such a tax and how much that tax should be. This law takes away their authority to decide whether to impose a sales tax on Internet transactions. This pre-emption of state authority to tax certain Internet services means that states are losing out on millions of dollars in revenue that they could invest in public services such as education, health care, and roads. States are losing $525 million each year as the result of untaxed Internet purchases, but the internet retail business grows rapidly each year, so this number will increase with time.[1]

What the law provides: In 2007, Pres. Bush signed this law that amends the Internet Tax Freedom Act to extend the moratorium on certain taxes relating to the Internet and electronic commerce. The moratorium applies to federal, state, and local governments and makes it illegal for them to tax internet transactions.

Internet sellers must collect sales taxes only in the few states where they have warehouses. Large corporations can take advantage of the no-internet tax policy by creating separate entities for their online stores and then keeping warehouses only in states without sales tax.[2]

What the law ignores:
  U.S. Constitution, General Welfare Clause, Art. I,§ 8, cl. 2.
  U.S. Constitution, Tenth Amendment: "The powers no delegated to the United States by the Constitution, nor prohibited by it

to the States, are reserved to the States respectively, or to the people."

What Congress can do: In 2009, Congressmembers can repeal the law and allow states to decide whether they want to impose taxes on commercial internet transactions.

See also: http://www.entrepreneur.com/tradejournals/article/ 171442402_2.html

---

[1] See study by Forrester Research Inc. cited in note 2.

[2] Howard Gleckman, *The Great Internet Tax Debate, Business Week,* http://www.businessweek.com/2000/00_13/b3674184.htm, (8/5/08).

VETERANS

Bush Law: Budget for Veterans Administration Treatment for Post-Traumatic Stress Disorder

Citation: 38 U. S. C. 301.

Who has been hurt by this Bush Law: Of the 1.5 million men and women who have served in Iraq and Afghanistan, approximately half a million troops are coming back to the U.S. with serious combat-related psychological wounds, including post-traumatic stress disorder (PTSD).[1] PTSD is "an anxiety disorder that can occur after you have been through a traumatic event... These events can include: combat or military exposure...terrorist attacks...sexual or physical assault..." and includes symptoms such as violent or aggressive behavior; drinking or drug problems; feeling of hopelessness, shame, or despair; flashbacks; feeling numb; fear for your safety and always feeling on guard; and many more.[2] PTSD is not a disorder that disappears or that someone can simply adjust to. World War II veteran, Tim Spiller, 88: "It never goes away, I have flashbacks all the time."[3] The Department of Veterans Affairs (VA) is under funded, understaffed and lacks facilities to treat veterans suffering from PTSD. Of the 1,400 VA hospitals, only 27 have PTSD outpatient programs.[4] Less than 40% of soldiers who seek PTSD treatment receive the medical care they need.[5] The VA is delaying veterans' claims for benefits, which causes further harm to veterans' mental health.[6] Veterans for Common Sense and Veterans United for Truth, Inc. filed a class action law suit against the VA and various VA officials and Alberto Gonzales in July 2007 raising all of these issues. Closing arguments were heard on May 1, 2008.[7]

What the law provides: 38 U. S. C. 301 states the VA's purpose: to distribute benefits, including health care, to veterans and their dependents. VA benefits cover both physical and medical conditions, including PTSD. Pres. Bush's federal budgets have consistently failed to commit enough money to the VA to adequately care for the estimated 500,000 veterans with PTSD.

What the law ignores:

U.S. Constitution, General Welfare Clause, Art. I,§ 8, cl. 2.
U.S. Constitution: Fifth Amendment.
U.N. Charter, Preamble.
U.N. Charter, Art. 55 and 56.
ICCPR, Preamble.
ICCPR, Art 23, Sec. 1.
ICERD, Art. 5.
ICAT, Art. 16, Sec. 1.

Bills proposed to undo the law:

Congressmembers proposed 19 bills, e.g. H.R. 3051 and S. 713, that give more funding to the VA specifically for PTSD-related issues that had not passed by Aug. 1, 2008.

What Congress can do: In 2009, Congressmembers should reintroduce and pass this legislation.

See also, e.g. MCLI website for comprehensive PTSD legislation and see Iraq and Afghanistan Veterans of America: http://www.iava.org/documents/Mental_Health.pdf

---

[1] Iraq and Afghanistan Veterans of America, http://www.iava.org/component/option,com_/Itemid,66/option,content/task,view/id,2414/ (6/10/08)

[2] National Center for PTSD, http://www.ncptsd.va.gov/ncmain/ncdocs/fact_shts/fs_what_is_ptsd.html (6/19/08).

[3] Joe Vargo, *Still Fighting War Stress, The Press-Enterprise*, 4/13/08. http://www.pe.com/localnews/inland/stories/PE_News_Local_D_iw014.3cb578d.html (6/9/08)

4 http://www.veteransptsdclassaction.org/pdf/courtfiled/
veteranscomplaint.pdf (6/9/08)

5 Defense Health Board Task Force on Mental Health, http://
www.health.mil/dhb/mhtf/MHTF-Report-Final.pdf (6/19/08).

6 Michelle Roberts, *Benefits delay puts soldiers at risk*, *Associated Press*,
6/17/08.

7 Laura Parker, *Lawsuit says VA mishandled claims*, *USA Today*, 5/20/
07.

Bush Law: Financing of Walter Reed Army Medical Center

Citation: Annual Department of Defense Appropriations Acts.

Who is hurt by this law: In February 2007, *The Washington Post* printed a series of articles on the sub-standard conditions and complicated bureaucracy at 113-acre Walter Reed Army Medical Center in Maryland. The facility houses patients with brain injuries, organ damage, severed limbs, and post-traumatic stress disorder. The articles described horrible conditions at one of the facilities known as Building 18. There are holes in floors and walls, mold-covered walls, cockroaches, rodent infestations, icy walkways, and at times, no heat or water.[1] Spanish-speaking patients and their families do not have adequate translators to communicate with the medical staff even though the Spanish-speaking soldiers were initially recruited in Spanish.[2] (*See also: Military Recruitment, Expedited Naturalization Executive Order,* p 110 and *National Defense Authorization Act of 2006,* p 116)

Walter Reed's bureaucracy is also extremely difficult to navigate. Patients must file 22 different documents with eight different commands and often their paperwork is lost, in part, because the Army's three personnel databases are incompatible with one another.[3]

What the law provides: Walter Reed is funded through the Department of Defense Appropriations Acts each year. In FY '08, military medical departments, including Walter Reed, faced budget cuts, or as the DoD calls them, "efficiency wedges," of $343 million out of a total budget of $2.7 billion.[4]

What the lack of financing ignores:
U.S. Constitution, General Welfare Clause, Art. I,§ 8, cl. 2.
U.N. Charter, Preamble.

U.N. Charter, Art. 55 & 56.
ICAT, Art. 16, §1.
ICCPR, Art. 23, §1.
ICERD, Art. 5.

What Congress can do: In 2009, Congress can increase the funding for Walter Reed Army Medical Center in the Department of Defense Appropriations Act.

---

[1] Dana Priest and Anne Hull, *Soldiers Face Neglect, Frustration At Army's Top Medical Facility, The Washington Post*, February 18, 2007.

[2] Id.

[3] Id.

[4] Vice Admiral Donald Arthur, Navy Surgeon General, House Hearing on Military Health Care, March 27, 2007, http://www.washingtonpost.com/wp-srv/nation/transcripts/military_healthcare_hearing032707.html (7/10/08).

Bush Law: Financing for the Department of Veterans Affairs Homeless Veterans Program

Citation: Annual appropriations bills for the Department of Veterans Affairs (VA).

Who is hurt by this law: There are over 200,000 homeless veterans on any given night and about 400,000 homeless at one point in a year.[1] According to the National Survey of Homeless Assistance Providers and Clients, veterans make up 23% of all homeless people in the U.S.,[2] having served in World War II, Korean War, Cold War, Vietnam War, Grenada, Panama, Lebanon, War in Iraq, and War in Afghanistan. The VA's homeless veteran programs serve 100,000 veterans each year, but with 400,000 homeless at one time over the course of a year, there are still 300,000 in need of assistance plus many more coming for longer recovery.[3] There are over 400 homeless veterans of the Iraq and Afghanistan wars already. VA and other aid groups believe that as soldiers return home, the numbers of homeless veterans from these wars will surge further.[4]

The VA's Homeless Providers Grant and Per Diem program gives money to community organizations that help veterans by providing services.[5] If Congress increased funding, these

132

community organizations that are vital in caring for homeless veterans would have more money and could provide more services to more veterans. Other VA programs, such as Domiciliary Care for Homeless Veterans, a Supported Housing Program with the Department of Housing and Urban Development, and the Loan Guarantee Program for Multifamily Traditional Housing would also greatly benefit from increased funding.[6]

What the law provides: The annual appropriations to the VA are not sufficient to provide assistance and housing to the 400,000 veterans who experience homelessness each year.

What the law ignores:

U.S. Constitution, General Welfare Clause, Art. I, §8, cl. 2.
U.N. Charter, Preamble.
U.N. Charter, Art. 55 & 56.
International Covenant on Civil and Political Rights (ICCPR), Preamble.
ICCPR, Art. 7.
ICAT, Art.16(1).

What Congress can do: In 2009, Congress can increase the funding for the Department of Veterans Affairs, specifically targeting their Homeless Veterans Program.

---

[1] National Coalition for Homeless Veterans, http://www.nchv.org/background.cfm, (7/10/08).

[2] U.S. Interagency Council on Homelessness and the Urban Institute, 1999.

[3] National Coalition for Homeless Veterans, http://www.nchv.org/background.cfm, (7/10/08).

[4] Erik Eckholm, Surge Seen in Number of Homeless Veterans, New York Times, Nov. 7, 2007.

[5] U.S. Department of Veterans Affairs, http://www1.va.gov/homeless/page.cfm?pg=3, (7/11/08).

[6] U.S. Department of Veterans Affairs, http://www1.va.gov/homeless/page.cfm?pg=2, (7/11/08).

WARS IN AFGHANISTAN, IRAQ AND ...

Bush "Law": Lack of Enforcement of Veterans Benefits

Citation: Uniformed Services Employment and Reemployment Rights Act (USERRA), 38 U.S.C. §4301, et. seq.

Who is hurt by this lack of enforcement: According to Sen. Edward Kennedy (D-MA), who held a hearing on veterans' employment issues, "tens of thousands of veterans returning home have faced the harsh reality that their service to our country has cost them the salary they deserve, their health care, and other benefits, and even jobs."[1] The hearing also released the data: nearly

134

11,000 service members were denied prompt reemployment when they returned from military service; more than 22,000 lost seniority, which affected their pay and other benefits; employers cut almost 20,000 pensions of service members returning to their jobs; nearly 11,000 did not get their health insurance back; and forty-four percent of National Guardsmen who filed USERRA complaints with the Department of Labor were dissatisfied with the way the Department handled their cases.[2]

What the law provides: USERRA "prohibits discrimination against persons because of their service in the Armed Forces Reserve, the National Guard, or other uniformed services...[and] prohibits an employer from denying any benefit of employment on the basis of an individual's membership, application for membership, performance of service, application for service, or obligation for service in the uniformed services...[and] protects the rights of veterans, reservists, National Guard members, and... other[s] to reclaim their civilian employment after being absent due to military service or training."[3] Enforcement, oversight, and implementation fall on the Department of Labor, Department of Defense, and the Office of Special Counsel.[4]

What law the lack of enforcement ignores:
U.S. Constitution, General Welfare Clause, Art. 1, §8, cl. 2.
U.N. Charter, Preamble.
U.N. Charter, Art. 55 & 56.
ICCPR, Preamble.
ICCPR, Art. 2(1).
ICERD, Art. 2.
ICERD, Art. 5 (e)(i-v).

Bill proposed to enforce the law:
S. 2471: USERRA Enforcement Improvement Act of 2007 (introduced 12/13/07); sponsored by Sen. Edward Kennedy (D-MA) with 3 cosponsors.

What Congress can do: In 2009, Congressmembers can reintroduce and pass S. 2471.

---

[1] Statement of Edward M. Kennedy "Protecting the Employment Rights of Those Who Protect the United States," Senate Help Committee, November 8, 2007, http://kennedy.senate.gov/newsroom/press_release.cfm?id=2d9f4728-1d7e-4fef-82eb-21b95ddde834, (7/11/08).

[2] Id.

[3] U.S. Office of Special Counsel, Uniformed Services Employment and Reemployment Rights Act, http://www.osc.gov/userra.htm, (7/11/08).

[4] Supra note 1.

Bush Law: Authorization for the Use of Military Force in Afghanistan (AUMF) of 2001

Citation: Public Law 107-40, 115 Stat. 225.

Who is hurt by this law: By July 2008 the war in Afghanistan has caused 541 reported deaths of U. S. soldiers and 331 reported deaths of coalition soldiers.[1] The U.S. government has not reported the total number of civilian casualties but in 2007, there were 430 civilian casualties and in 2008, from January through June, there were 698.[2] Over 100,000 people have had to flee their homes because of the violence.[3] In a speech in November, 2001, Pres. Bush stated that one reason for going to war in Afghanistan was to "hunt down the members of the Al Qaeda organization who murdered innocent Americans."[4] Seven years later neither the CIA nor the U.S. military have actually apprehended Osama bin Laden. The U.S. says one of its present goals in Afghanistan is to stabilize the region and remove remaining Taliban forces, but the local police forces have done little to stop opium trafficking, a lucrative business controlled by insurgents.[5] According to the United Nations Office on Drugs and Crime "2008 World Drug Report," production of opium, the base ingredient in heroine, is on the rise and Afghanistan had a record opium harvest in 2007.[6]

Bush's War on Terror and the expansion of the executive branch are based on the AUMF and he has cited it as authority for many of his defense and security policies, including military commissions and electronic surveillance.[7] (*See also:* Suspension of Habeas Corpus, The USA PATRIOT Act, and FISA.)

What the law provides: §2(a): "In General.—That the President is authorized to use all necessary and appropriate force against those nations, organizations, or persons he determines planned, authorized, committed, or aided the terrorist attacks that occurred on September 11, 2001, or harbored such organizations or persons, in order to prevent any future acts of international terrorism against the United States by such nations, organizations, or persons."

What the law ignores:

U.S. Constitution, Preamble: "We the People, of the United States, in Order to form a more perfect Union, establish Justice, insure domestic Tranquility, provide for the common defense, promote the general Welfare, and secure the Blessings of Liberty to ourselves and our Posterity, do ordain and establish this Constitution for the United States of America."

U.S. Constitution, General Welfare Clause, Art. 1, §8, cl. 2.

U.S. Constitution, Art. I, §8, cl. 1 & 11: "The Congress shall have Power...To declare war..."

U.N. Charter, Art. 2(4).

U.N. Charter, Art. 1: "The Purposes of the United Nations are: (1) To maintain international peace and security, and to that end: to take effective collective measures for the prevention and removal of threats to the peace, and for the suppression of acts of aggression or other breaches of the peace, and to bring about by peaceful means, and in conformity with the principles of justice and international law, adjustment or settlement of international disputes or situations which might lead to a breach of the peace."

U.N. Charter, Art. 33(1): "The parties to any dispute, the continuance of which is likely to endanger the maintenance of international peace and security, shall, first of all, seek a solution by negotiation, enquiry, mediation, conciliation, arbitration, judicial settlement, resort to regional agenciesor arrangements, or other peaceful means of their own choice."

U.N. Charter, Art. 37: "(1) Should the parties to a dispute of the nature referred to in Article 33 fail to settle it by the means indicated in that Article, they shall refer it to the Security Council. (2) If the Security Council deems that the continuance of the dispute is in fact likely to endanger the maintenance of international peace and security, it shall decide whether to take action under Article 36 or to recommend such terms of settlement as it may consider appropriate."

U.N. Charter, Art. 39: "The Security Council shall determine the existence of any threat to the pace, breach of the peace, or act of aggression and shall make recommendations, or decide what measures shall be taken in accordance with Articles 41 and 42, to maintain or restore international peace and security."

What Congress can do: Congress can repeal the AUMF of 2001.

See also: Amnesty International, http://thereport.amnesty.org/ eng/Regions/Asia-Pacific/Afghanistan

---

[1] Iraq Coalition Casualty Count, icasualities.org/oef, (7/3/08).

[2] Afghan Civilian Deaths Rise Sharply in 2008, CNN, June 29, 2008, http://www.cnn.com/2008/WORLD/asiapcf/06/29/afghanistan/, (6/7/ 08).

[3] Amnesty International, http://www.amnesty.org/en/library/asset/ ASA11/006/2007/en/dom-ASA110062007en.html, (6/7/08).

[4] President George W. Bush, Speech at the Georgia World Congress Center in Atlanta on November 8, 2001, http://archives.cnn.com/2001/ US/11/08/rec.bush.transcript/, (7/3/08).

[5] Aryn Baker and Kajaki Olya, Afghanistan: A War That's Still Not Won, Time Magazine, June 26, 2008.

[6] United Nations Office on Drugs and Crime, 2008 World Drug Report, June 2008, http://reliefweb.int/rw/lib.nsf/db900sid/MUMA-7G39VW/ $file/unodc-worldreport2008.pdf?openelement, (7/2/08)

[7] Jacob Weisberg, The Power-Madness of King George, Slate Magazine, January 25, 2006.

Bush Law: Authorization for the Use of Military Force Against Iraq Resolution of 2002 (AUMF 2002)

Citation: Public Law 107-243, 116 Stat. 1498.

Who is hurt by this law: As of July 2008, over 4,138 U.S. soldiers have been killed fighting in Iraq and there have been over 30,324 U.S. military members wounded[1] and at least 500,000 veterans of the Iraq war have Post Traumatic Stress Disorder.[2] At least 1,123 U.S. contractors have also died.[3] The number of civilian Iraqi deaths due to the war is somewhere between 85,323[4] and 655,000.[5] There are another 2,000,000 Iraqi refugees, the third-largest refugee population world-wide, and another 2,000,000 are internally displaced from their homes within Iraq.[6] Coalition deaths number over 4,452.[7] The war has also cost U.S. taxpayers over $531,589,000,000.[8]

Rep. Dennis Kucinich's (D-OH) articles of impeachment charge that Pres. Bush misled the U.S. and Members of Congress to believe that Iraq possessed weapons of mass destruction, attempted to link

138

the 9/11 attacks to Saddam Hussein and Iraq, and misrepresented Iraq as an imminent threat to the U.S.[9] Rep. Kucinich also introduced articles of impeachment in 2007 against Vice President Dick Cheney, who "actively and systematically sought to deceive the citizens and Congress...about an alleged threat of Iraqi weapons of mass destruction..." and "purposely manipulated the intelligence process to deceive the citizens and Congress...about an alleged relationship between Iraq and al Qaeda to justify the use of the...Armed Forces against the nation of Iraq in a manner damaging to our national security interests..."[10]

In 2004, the CIA's Iraq Survey Group (ISG) issued a report that they had "not found evidence that Saddam possessed WMD stocks in 2003..." and that "the problem of discerning WMD in Iraq is highlighted by the pre-war misapprehensions of weapons which were not there."[11] A study by the Institute for Defense Analyses "found no 'smoking gun' (i.e., direct connection) between Saddam's Iraq and al Qaeda."[12]

Retired General Anthony Zinni charges that "there was dereliction in insufficient forces being put on the ground and fully understanding the dimensions of the plan. I think there was dereliction in lack of planning..."[13]

What the law provides: §3(a): "Authorization.—The President is authorized to use the Armed Forces of the United States as he determines to be necessary and appropriate in order to—(1) defend the national security of the United States against the continuing threat posed by Iraq; and (2) enforce all relevant United Nations Security Council resolutions regarding Iraq."

What the law ignores:
  U.S. Constitution, Preamble.
  U.S. Constitution, General Welfare Clause, Art. 1, §8, cl. 1.
  U.S. Constitution, Art. I, §8, cl. 1 & 11.
  U.S. Constitution, Art. II, §1, cl. 8: Oath of office.
  U.S. Constitution, Art. II, §3.
  U.N. Charter, Art. 2(4): "All Members shall give the United Nations every assistance in any action it takes in accordance with the present Charter, and shall refrain from giving assistance to any state against which the United Nations is taking preventive or enforcement action."
  U.N. Charter, Art. 1.
  U.N. Charter, Art. 33(1).

U.N. Charter, Art. 37(1) .
U.N. Charter, Art. 39.

Bills proposed to repeal the AUMF in 110th Congress include (see website for Senate and House bills to reduce troop numbers):

S.J.Res. 15: United States Policy in Iraq Resolution of 2007 (introduced 5/25/2007); sponsored by Sen. Joseph Biden (D-DE).

H.R. 930: Military Success in Iraq and Diplomatic Surge for National and Political Reconciliation in Iraq Act of 2007 (introduced 2/8/2007); sponsored by Rep. Sheila Jackson-Lee (D-TX).

H.R. 5507: Fully-Funded United States Military Redeployment and Sovereignty of Iraq Restoration Act of 2008 (introduced 2/27/2008); sponsored by Rep. Lynn Woolsey (D-CA) with 20 cosponsors.

H.J.Res. 18: To Redeploy U.S. Forces from Iraq (introduced 1/17/2007); sponsored by Rep. John Murtha (D-PA) with 103 cosponsors, incl. Rep. Barbara Lee (D-CA), Cochair, Progressive Caucus.

H.R. 413: To repeal the Authorization for the Use of Military Force Against Iraq Resolution of 2002 (introduced 1/11/2007); sponsored by Rep. Sam Farr (D-CA) with 9 cosponsors.

H.R. 3938: Bring Our Troops Home Responsibly Act of 2007 (introduced 10/23/2007); sponsored by Rep. John Dingell (D-MI) with 7 cosponsors.

H.R. 2450: To repeal the Authorization for the Use of Military Force Against Iraq Resolution of 2002 (introduced 5/23/2007); sponsored by Rep. Ellen Tauscher (D-CA).

H.R. 1292: To repeal the Authorization for the Use of Military Force Against Iraq Resolution of 2002 (introduced 3/1/2007); sponsored by Rep. John Larson (D-CT).

H.R. 2605: Sunset of Public Law 107-243 Act of 2007 (introduced 6/7/2007); sponsored by Rep. Ronald Paul (R-TX) with 23 cosponsors.

What Congress can do: Immediately in 2009, Congressmembers can reintroduce and pass the 110th Congress' bills that would repeal the AUMF and other bills that require a redeployment date for all troops in Iraq.

See also: Iraq Coalition Casualty Count, icasualties.org

[1] www.icasualties.org , (7/24/08).

[2] Iraq and Afghanistan Veterans of America, http://www.iava.org/component/option,com_/Itemid,66/option,content/task,view/id,2414/, (6/10/08).

[3] David Ivanovich, Contractor Deaths up 17 percent across Iraq in 2007, Houston Chronicle, 2/9/2008.

[4] www.iraqbodycount.org , (6/30/08).

[5] Johns Hopkins School of Public Health, Updated Iraq Affirms Earlier Mortality Estimates, 10/11/2006, http://www.jhsph.edu/publichealthnews/press_releases/2006/burnham_iraq_2006.html, (7/1/08).

[6] Continuing Challenges in Iraq, In & Around the UN, June 2008.

[7] www.icasualties.org/oif , (6/30/08).

[8] See Department of Defense Budget for the Wars in Iraq and Afghanistan, p. 145.

[9] Dennis Kucinich, H.Res. 1258, Art. II, III, and IV.

[10] Dennis Kucinich, H.Res. 333 Art. I(1).

[11] Report concludes no WMD in Iraq, BBC News, 10/7/2004, http://news.bbc.co.uk/2/hi/middle_east/3718150.stm,, (6/30/08).

[12] Institute for Defense Analyses, Iraqi Perspectives Project; Saddam and Terrorism: Emerging Insights from Captured Iraqi Documents, Volume 1, P. ES-1 11/2007.

[13] Gen. Anthony Zinni, Tom Clancy, and Tony Koltz, Battle Ready, C.P. Commanders, Inc., 2004.

Bush "Law": Status of Forces Agreements (SOFAs)

Citation: E.g. Treaties and Other International Acts (T.I.A.S.) Exchange of notes (between Afghanistan and the U. S.)[1] with Afghanistan, et al. Entered into force May 28, 2003.

Who is hurt by this "law": The nations that house U.S. military bases are threatened by the constant U. S. military presence on their soil and the peoples of the United States are less safe because of them. These bases "stretch our military beyond its capabilities, bringing about fiscal insolvency and very possibly doing mortal damage to our republican institutions," according to Chalmers Johnson.[2]

Currently the U.S. has SOFAs with over 100 nations[3] and approximately 760 bases world-wide,[4] allowing U.S. military to maintain a foreign presence across the globe. Twenty-five of these

141

agreements, including one with Afghanistan, have been concluded since Bush-Cheney took office in 2001.[5] They are currently attempting to negotiate a SOFA with Iraq, which means that even if the newly elected president ends the war, a contingent of military forces will remain in Iraq.[6] If agreed upon, it will "preserve the right of U.S. forces to initiate unilateral military action and continue rounding up tens of thousands of Iraqis in abusive preventive detention facilities where human rights are violated routinely," according to Tom Hayden.[7]

These SOFAs are also dangerous to the peoples of the U. S. because they spread our military thin. If the U.S. were to suffer an invasion or attack, it would be more difficult to defend the country from abroad. Also, in Italy, more than 70,000 protestors marched through the city of Vicenzain 2007 to show their objections to the expansion of a U.S. military base.[8] The protestors said that they did not want the base there at all because they believe Americans cause trouble and that in case of military conflict, the base, which is at the heart of the city, could become a target.[9] There have been similar protests in South Korea.[10] In the Philippines, as in many other developing countries, the SOFAs provide that the "host" country supply the logistical support necessary for the U.S. military to maintain their forces in the region, spare parts, transportation, communication, medical services, and many more.[11]

The constant presence of a military base in a foreign nation is essentially a threat against the territorial integrity and political independence of a nation. Having a U.S. military presence in so many countries creates what the CIA calls "blowback," or the unintended consequences of military action. Such a presence could result in future terrorist attacks on the U.S. or U.S. bases on foreign soil.

What the "law" provides: Status of Forces Agreements (SOFAs) are stand-alone agreements between the U.S. and other nations that allow the U.S. to station military forces in those foreign nations. These agreements are signed by the president, but do not have to be approved by the Senate as treaties do. Every SOFA is different, but most of them define the legal status of the U.S. Armed Forces while operating abroad and address which of the laws apply to military forces while they are within that nation.[12]

142

What the "law" ignores:

U.S. Constitution, General Welfare Clause, Art. I,§ 8, cl. 2.

U.N. Charter, Art. 2(1).

U.N. Charter, Art. 2(4).

U.N. Charter, Art. 55 & 56.

What Congress can do: In 2009, Congressmembers can:

Stop all funding of foreign military bases; and

Resolve that present Status of Forces Agreements do not have the approval of Congress.

See also: Department of Defense's Base Structure Report Fiscal Year 2008 Baseline, http://www.acq.osd.mil/ie/irm/irm_library/ BSR2008Baseline.pdf, (7/25/08).

---

[1] For a complete list of SOFAs, see, http://assets.opencrs.com/rpts/ RL34531_20080616.pdf (7/25/08).

[2] Chalmers Johnson, America's Empire of Bases, TomDispatch.com, Jan. 15, 2005, http://www.tomdispatch.com/post/1181/chalmers_johnson_ on_garrisoning_the_planet, (7/25/08).

[3] Congressional Research Service, Status of Forces Agreement (SOFA): What Is It, and How Might One Be Utilized in Iraq?, June 16, 2008.

[4] Department of Defense, Base Structure Report, FY 2008, http:// www.acq.osd.mil/ie/irm/irm_library/BSR2008Baseline.pdf, (7/25/08).

[5] Supra note 3.

[6] Tom Hayden, Secret US-Iraq "Status of Forces" Agreement Would Preserve Human Rights Violations, Torture Policies in Iraq, Huffington Post, July 8, 2008, http://www.huffingtonpost.com/tom-hayden/secret- us-iraq-status-of_b_111456.html, (7/24/08).

[7] Id.

[8] Lisa Jucca, Italians Protest Over U.S. Base Expansion, Reuters, Feb. 17, 2007.

[9] Id.

[10] Natasha Persaud, U.S. Base Expansion in Korea Sparks Protests, Socialism & Liberation Magazine, Aug. 2006.

[11] Sara Flounders, Expansion of U.S. Bases Spur Philippine Resistance, International Action Center, Mar. 29, 2008.

[12] Supra note 3.

Bush-Cheney "law": Statement on Signing the Ronald Reagan National Defense Authorization Act, 2005

Citation: Ronald Reagan National Defense Authorization Act, 2005, 40 Weekly Comp. Pres. Doc. 2673 (Oct 29, 2004).

Who is hurt by this "law": The Congress and everyone concerned about maintaining three equal branches of government is hurt by Bush's Signing Statement. Also hurt are the majority of members of Congress who felt it necessary to prevent fraudulent government contracts for reconstruction of Iraq by appointing a Special Inspector General as a condition for passing Bush's requested funding for Iraq.

What the "law" provides: Pres. Bush's Signing Statement rejected the independence of the proposed OIG and directed that the "Special Inspector General shall refrain from initiating, carrying out, or completing an audit or investigation, or from issuing a subpoena, which requires access to sensitive operation plans, intelligence matters, counter-intelligence matters, ongoing criminal investigations by administrative units of the Department of Defense related to national security, or other matters the disclosure of which would constitute a serious threat to national security."

What the "law" ignores:

U.S. Constitution, Art. 1, §7, cl. 2: The President shall either approve and sign a bill or veto it and return it to Congress, which can decide to override his veto. *See: Clinton v. City of New York*, 524 U.S. 417 (1998), invalidating the line item veto.

What Congress can do: In 2009, Congress can: (1) act on Sen. Arlen Specter's (R-PA) legislation (first proposed in 2006 as the Presidential Signing Statements Act, S. 3731, 109th Cong.) that would instruct the federal courts to disregard signing statements and provide standing to Members of Congress who wish to challenge such statements in court; (2) pass legislation clarifying that signing statements, including this one, do not alter the requirements of the law being signed; (3) refuse to confirm any nominees for office until it is clear that they understands that their duty is to the law as passed by Congress and signed by the President, without regard to signing statements or other maneuvers.

144

Bush "Law": Department of Defense (DOD) Budget for the Wars in Afghanistan and Iraq

Citation: Department of Defense Appropriations Act of 2008, Public Law 110-116 (and all previous years) and Supplemental and Emergency Appropriations Acts to fund the wars in Afghanistan and Iraq.[1]

Who is hurt by this "law": With the cost of oil rising, the sub-prime mortgage crisis, and the economy generally in a recession, Pres. Bush cut the budget for domestic economic issues in favor of waging undeclared wars in Afghanistan and Iraq. He has spent over $531,589,000,000. in U.S. taxpayer's money as of June, 2008.[2] So far it has cost $341,400,000. per day, $4,681. per household, and $1,721. per person.[3] The U.S. economy and taxpayers are suffering domestically. This money could have been used to pay for 8,638,014 elementary school teachers each year; provided 154,997,406 people with health care; given 231,791,436 children health care coverage each year; provided 4,090,926 affordable housing units; or provided 81,307,978 scholarships for university students for one year.[4] With a national debt of $9,400,000,000,000[5] and ongoing debts to countries all over the world, the money spent on the war in Iraq could also have been used to pay off a portion of this debt.[6]

The U.S. also owes the United Nations $846,000,000 in dues as of May 7, 2008.[7] According to the National Priorities Project, this money would be better spent on preventative national security measures that do not involve waging war, such as "securing nuclear materials abroad and participating in multi-lateral diplomatic and peacekeeping operations; ...[and] homeland security such as providing port security and coordinating emergency first responders;.."[8]

What the "law" provides: The Bush Administration has been funding the wars in Afghanistan and Iraq in several ways:

A Department of Defense Appropriations Act every year since 2003.[9]

Supplemental appropriations acts to further provide monetary support for the war in Iraq. These often piggyback on funding for other politically popular—and often necessary—issues such as tsunami relief.[10] Title I, Chapter 2 of H.R. 4939 gives emergency supplemental appropriations to the Iraq Security Forces Fund, and provides hurricane disaster relief.[11]

What the "law" ignores:

U.S. Constitution, Preamble.
U.S. Constitution, General Welfare Clause, Art. 1, § 8, cl. 1.
U.S. Constitution, Art. I, § 8, cl. 1 & 11.
U.S. Constitution, Art. I, § 8, cl. 1 & 12.
U.N. Charter, Preamble.
U.N. Charter, Art. 1.
U.N. Charter, Art. 2(3).
U.N. Charter, Art. 2(4).
U.N. Charter, Art. 55 and 56.

What Congress can do: In 2009, Congress can discontinue funding the wars in Afghanistan and Iraq through both supplemental appropriations acts and the annual DoD appropriations acts.

See also: National Priorities Project, www.nationalpriorities.org

---

[1] See, H.R. 3222, H.R. 5631, H.R. 2863, H.R. 4613, and H.R. 2658.See also, H.R. 4939, H.R. 1268, H.R. 2863, et. al.

[2] National Priorities Project, http://www.nationalpriorities.org/costofwar_home, (6/26/08).

[3] Id.

[4] National Priorities Project, http://www.nationalpriorities.org/tradeoffs, (6/30/08).

[5] http://www.federalbudget.com/, (6/26/08).

[6] U.S. Dept. of the Treasury, http://www.treas.gov/tic/mfh.txt, (6/28/08).

[7] Warren Sach, Assistant-Secretary-General, Controller, United Nations, Financial Presentation: UN Cash Position, 5/9/2008, http://www.un.org/ga/fifth/sach.un.cash.status.05.08.pdf, (7/1/08).

[8] National Priorities Project, http://www.nationalpriorities.org/national_security, (6/30/08).

[9] See, H.R. 4613, H.R. 2605, H.R. 2863.

[10] See, H.R. 2863, Department of Defense, Emergency Supplemental Appropriations to Address Hurricanes in the Gulf of Mexico, and Pandemic Influenza Act, 2006, H.R. 1268, Emergency Supplemental Appropriations Act for Defense, the Global War on Terror, and Tsunami Relief, 2005, and others.

[11] H.R. 4939,Emergency Supplemental Appropriations Act for Defense, the Global War on Terror, and Hurricane Recovery

Bush "Law": Outsourcing the Wars in Afghanistan and Iraq to Civilian Contractors

Citation: Department of Defense Appropriations Act of 2008 (Public Law 110-116).

Who is hurt by this "law": U.S. taxpayers are over-paying billions of dollars to private military companies (PMCs): e.g., Blackwater, Kellogg Brown and Root (KBR), and Dyncorp. The total cost of the war in Iraq is $539,000,000,000 as of July 2008. The Office of Inspector General (OIG) reported to Congress that the Pentagon couldn't account for nearly $15,000,000,000 for reconstruction in Iraq. The OIG also reported that there is no documentation for billions of dollars paid to contractors for telephones, trucks, etc.[1] The Department of Defense (DoD) paid $32 million to contractors to build the Iraqi military a new facility, but it was never built and no explanation has been given. The resources and Pentagon staff in charge of ensuring that the money is spent efficiently has not been increased.[2]

Latin Americans are hurt by the contracting business because companies, (e.g. Blackwater's affiliate, Greystone Limited), are recruiting security guards in countries throughout Latin America.[3] Many have combat experience and are willing to work for far less than their U.S. counterparts.[4]

This "law" hurts U.S. taxpayers as the Pentagon has become increasingly reliant on PMCs. In more than half of 21 DoD offices that the Government Accounting Office (GAO) investigated, private contractors outnumbered DoD employees. In Iraq, PMCs do work similar to that of soldiers—building and operating bases, interrogating prisoners, guarding convoys—but are paid much more.[5]

What the "law" provides: The annual DoD Appropriations Acts are funding the wars in Iraq and Afghanistan, as are the Supplemental Appropriations Acts since 2002. Under the "cost plus" contracts, civilian contractors have an incentive to increase spending because these contracts provide that the U.S. reimburses the contracting company for all its expenses, **plus** a percentage of those expenses. (If a company spends $1 million to build a housing facility and has a contract to receive 2% of those costs, the company would make $20,000. If it spends $10 million to build, their profits increase to $200,000).

Many of the contracts are "no-bid" or "sole source" contracts only offered to one company. With no competition the civilian contractor can charge as much as it wants, paid for by U.S. taxpayers. These contracts are permitted under U.S. law.[6] The Bush Administration cites "national security" as its reason for these contracts; they are quicker to negotiate and beneficial in a time of war. Before the U.S. invaded Iraq, the U.S. awarded a $7 billion no-bid contract to KBR, an affiliate of Halliburton, whose former CEO, Dick Cheney, served as U. S. Vice President (2001-2008).

What the "law" ignores:

U.S. Constitution, General Welfare Clause, Art. I, §8, cl. 2.

U.S. Constitution, Art. I, §8, cl. 1 & 12: "The Congress shall have power...To raise and support armies, but no Appropriation of Money to that Use shall be for a longer Term than two Years."

U.N. Charter, Preamble.

U.N. Charter, Art. 1.

U.N. Charter, Art. 2(3).

U.N. Charter, Art. 2(a).

U.N. Charter, Art. 55 and 56.

Bills proposed to undo the law:

H.R. 897: Iraq and Afghanistan Contractor Sunshine Act (introduced 2/7/07); sponsored by Rep. Janice Schakowsky (D-IL) with 61 cosponsors.

H.R. 4102: Stop Outsourcing Security Act (introduced 12/7/07); sponsored by Rep. Janice Schakowsky (D-IL) with 28 cosponsors.

S. 2398: Stop Outsourcing Security Act (introduced 11/16/07); sponsored by Sen. Bernard Sanders (I-VT) with 1 cosponsor.

What Congress can do: In 2009, Congressmembers can:

Reintroduce and pass H.R. 897;

Reintroduce and pass H.R. 4102/S. 2398;

Pass additional legislation that would prohibit no-bid contracts and cost-plus contracts in Iraq and Afghanistan.

---

[1] Frida Berrigan, *Trouble at the Pentagon, Common Dreams News Center*, June 12, 2008.

[2] Id.

[3] Id.

[4] Eric Stoner, *Outsourcing the Iraq War:Mercenary Recruiters Turn to*

Latin America, Common Dreams News Center, July 14, 2008.
[5] Supra, note 1.
[6] 48 CFR Ch. 1, Part 6.

Bush "Law": Criminal Immunity of Civilian Contractors in Afghanistan and Iraq

(*See also*: Outsourcing the Wars in Iraq and Afghanistan to Civilian Contractors)

Citation: Coalition Provisional Authority, Order 17 and the Military Extraterritorial Jurisdiction Act (MEJA), 18 U.S.C. §3261.

Who is hurt by this "law": The Iraqi people are hurt by the existence of Order 17 and the Department of Justice's lack of enforcement of MEJA because this combination effectively gives civilian contractors immunity from prosecution from both Iraqi and U.S. courts. There are an estimated 180,000 private contractors in Iraq[1] and thousands more in Afghanistan and they do a variety of jobs such as providing military training, food, and security for U.S. officials.

These contractors have been linked to numerous civilian deaths and incidents of abuse. On September 15, 2007,Blackwater employees opened fired on Iraqi civilians in Baghdad's Nisoor Square, killing 17. No one has been held accountable for these deaths.[2] In over 80% of the shooting incidents involving Blackwater, its employees fired the first shot.[3] Contractors from CACI International and Titan have been linked to torture and abuse at Abu Ghraib prison in Afghanistan.[4] Zapata Engineering employees were detained by the U.S. Marines after allegedly "repeatedly firing weapons at civilians and Marines, erratic driving, and possession of illegal weapons."[5] These contractors lost their jobs, but were never prosecuted.[6]

What the "law" provides: The Supreme Court held in *Reid v. Covert* that military courts, and thus the UCMJ, do not have jurisdiction over civilians in a time of peace.[7] Congress never declared war on Iraq, so the UCMJ does not apply to civilian contractors in Iraq. In 2007, Sen. Lindsey Graham (R-SC) inserted a five-word provision into a spending bill[8] that would make civilian contractors liable under the Uniform Code of Military Justice (UCMJ), but it has only been used once and even then, the incident involved a Candian-Iraqi translator in an assault on another contractor, not on an Iraqi civilian.[9]

MEJA was passed in 2000 and permits the prosecution of persons "employed by or accompanying the armed forces." Under MEJA, civilian contractors in Iraq could be held liable for crimes they commit, but no private contractor has ever been prosecuted under MEJA for abuses against Iraqi civilians.

The contractors are immune to Iraqi law due to Order 17 of the U.S.-led Coalition Provisional Authority (CPA). This Order issued in 2004, states: "contractors shall be immune from Iraqi legal process with respect to acts performed by them pursuant to the terms and conditions of a Contract or any sub-contract thereto."[10] It also defines contractors as "non-Iraqi legal entities or individuals not normally resident in Iraq, including their non-Iraqi employees."[11]

What the "law" ignores:

U.S. Constitution, General Welfare Clause, Art. I, §8, cl. 1.
U.S. Constitution, Art. I, § 8, cl. 1, 11 & 12.
U.N. Charter, Preamble.
U.N. Charter, Art. 1.
U.N. Charter, Art. 2(3)(4).
U.N. Charter, Art. 55 and 56.
ICAT, Art. 2(2).
ICAT, Art. 5(1)(b).
ICAT, Art. 16(1).
ICERD, Art. 5.

Bills proposed to undo the "law":

H.R. 2740: MEJA Expansion and Enforcement Act of 2007 (introduced 6/15/07; passed House 10/4/07); sponsored by Rep. David Price (D-NC) with 15 cosponsors.

S. 674: Transparency and Accountability in Military and Security Contracting Act of 2007 (introduced 2/16/07); sponsored by Sen. Barack Obama (D-IL) with 4 cosponsors.

What Congress can do: In 2009, Congressmembers can reintroduce and pass H.R. 2740 and S. 674.

See also: Human Rights First, *Private Security Contractors at War: Ending the Culture of Impunity,* 2008, http://www.humanri ghtsfirst.info/pdf/08115-usls-psc-final.pdf.

---

[1] T. Christian Miller, *Contractors Outnumber Troops in Iraq, Los Angeles Times,* July 4, 2007.

[2] Human Rights Watch, *Iraq: Pass New Law Ending Immunity for Contractors*, Jan. 9, 2008, http://hrw.org/english/docs/2008/01/09/iraq17703.htm, (7/24/08).

[3] Jomana Karadsheh, Zain Verjee, and Suzanne Simons, *Blackwater Most Often Shoots First, Congressional Report Says, CNN*, Oct. 2, 2007.

[4] Kathy Benz, *Lawsuit Targets Abu Ghraib Contractors, CNN,* July 24, 2007.

[5] Josh White and Griff Witte, *Tension, Confusion Between Troops, Contractors in Iraq, Washington Post,* July 10, 2005, http://www.washingtonpost.com/wp-dyn/content/article/2005/07/09/AR2005070901175.html (7/24/08).

[6] Josh White and Griff Witte, *Navy Won't File Charges in Iraqi Contractor Fracas, Washington Post,* March 25, 2006, http://www.washingtonpost.com/wp-dyn/content/article/2006/03/24/AR2006032401840.html, (7/24/08).

[7] *Reid v. Covert*, 345 U.S. 1, (1957).

[8] John Warner National Defense Authorization Act for Fiscal Year 2007, Pub. L. 109-364.

[9] Peter Graff, *U.S. Military Charges Civilian Contractor in Iraq, Common Dream News Center,* April 5, 2008.

[10] Human Rights Watch, *Iraq: Pass New Law Ending Immunity for Contractors*, Jan. 9, 2008, http://hrw.org/english/docs/2008/01/09/iraq17703.htm, (7/24/08).

[11] Human Rights Watch, Order 17.

Bush Signing Statement as Commander-in-Chief on U.S. Combat Activity in Colombia

Citation: Signing Statement on the Intelligence Authorization Act, 2005, 40 Weekly Comp. Pres. Doc. 3012 (Dec. 23, 2004).

Who is hurt by this Signing Statement: All of the members of Congress who voted for the Act to forbid combat operations in Colombia except in self-defense and to limit the number of U.S. troops to be stationed there are hurt because they saw their constitutional power violated.

All of the citizens of the U.S. concerned about U.S. operations in Colombia, and concerned about the 3-branch system of government under the U.S. Constitution, are hurt by this Signing Statement.

What the Signing Statement provides: "Section 502 of the Intelligence Authorization Act purports to place restrictions on use of the U.S. Armed Forces and other personnel in certain operations. The executive branch shall construe the restrictions in that section as advisory in nature, so that the provisions are consistent with the President's constitutional authority as Commander in Chief, including for the conduct of intelligence operations, and to supervise the unitary executive branch.".

What the "law" ignores:

Intelligence Authorization Act for Fiscal Year 2005, §§105, 107 & 305, Public Law No. 108-147, 118 Stat. 3939.

U.S. Constitution, Art. I, Sec. 7, Cl. 2, requiring the President to either approve and sign a bill or return it to Congress for consideration of an override of his veto (with no provision for contradictory signing statements). See also *Clinton v. City of New York,* 524 U.S. 417 (1998) (invalidating the line-item veto).

U.S. Constitution, Art. II, Sec. 3, requiring that the President "shall take Care that the Laws be faithfully executed."

What Congress can do: (1) act on legislation (first proposed by Sen. Arlen Specter (R-PA) in 2006 as the Presidential Signing Statements Act, S. 3731, 109th Cong.) instructing the federal courts to disregard signing statements and provide standing to Members of Congress who wish to challenge such statements in court; (2) pass legislation clarifying that signing statements, including this one, do not alter the requirements of the law; (3) refuse to confirm nominees for office until it is clear that they understand that their duty is to the law as passed by Congress and signed by the President without regard to signing statements.

Contributor: Prof. Zachary Wolfe, George Washington University

2008 ECONOMIC CRISIS

Bush Laws: Commodity Futures Modernization Act (Dec. 14, 2000)[1] and Bankruptcy Abuse Prevention and Consumer Protection Act (Apr. 20, 2005)[2]

A Little History:

Congress passed a series of laws, starting in 1913, creating a national banking system, and the **Federal Trade Commission Act (1914)** prohibiting unfair or deceptive business practices. During the Great Depression, Congress passed the **Glass Steagall Act of 1933** (a.k.a. Banking Act) as an emergency response to: 1) prohibit commercial banks (focusing on consumer activities such as checking and savings) from engaging in the investment business (dealing with speculative trading and mergers); 2) gave the Federal Reserve System tighter regulation of national banks; 3) prohibited bank sales of securities; and 4) created the Federal Deposit Insurance Corporation (FDIC), to insure bank deposits with a pool of money appropriated from banks.[3]

After the Depression, Congress passed the **Truth in Lending Act (1968)**[4] requiring banks to disclose loan terms & fees. "To assure a meaningful disclosure of credit terms so that the consumer will be able to compare more readily the various credit terms available to him and avoid the uninformed use of credit, and to protect the consumer against inaccurate and unfair credit billing and credit card practices."[5]

LAWS WHICH WEAKENED GLASS-STEAGALL ACT

- **Bank Holding Company Act Amendments (1970)**[6]
- **Garn-St. Germain Depository Institutions Act (1982)**[7]

153

- **Federal Deposit Insurance Corporation Improvement Act (1991)**[8]
- **Truth in Lending Act "Reform" (Sept. 30, 1995)**[9]
- **Gramm-Leach-Bliley Act (1999)**[10]
- **Commodity Futures Modernization Act (Dec. 14, 2000)**

Bankruptcy Abuse Prevention and Consumer Protection Act (Apr. 20, 2005)

Who is hurt by these Bush laws: Everyone who works for a living and is paid wages. Everyone who was relying on good laws from the New Deal: Eight decades ago the economy was rampant in speculations, tax breaks for the rich, and weak labor unions, similar to the 2000s when Bush provided tax cuts for the wealthy (see Taxes, pg. 121), financing two wars (see Wars, pg. 134), causing mortgage foreclosures (see Housing, pg. 85), and failing to enforce the Fair Labor Standards Act (see Labor, pg. 100), and passing deregulation laws that have swept the U.S. economy into a deep hole even with the bailout.

Credit default swaps (CDSs) are essentially insurance policies covering the losses on securities in the event of a default. Because of the swap-related provisions of Gramm's bill—which were supported by Fed chairman Alan Greenspan and Treasury Secretary Larry Summers—a $62 trillion market (nearly four times the size of the entire US stock market) remained utterly unregulated, meaning no one made sure the banks and hedge funds had the assets to cover the losses they guaranteed.[11] "Since then, big hedge funds and other traders discovered that swaps could be traded and used to speculate on how close a company was to collapse. The market mushroomed. Its total value outgrew that of all publicly traded stocks combined. The swaps market began to affect the financial system in once unimagined ways."[12] Between 1994 and 2004, subprime mortgage lending grew from $35 billion to $530 billion.[13]

What Congress can do: In 2009, Congress can repeal these deregulation laws and reinstate laws that were set in place to protect workers and small investors from another catastrophic Great Depression.

[1] Public Law 106-554, §1(a)(5).

[2] Public Law 109-8, 119 Stat. 23.

[3] http://law.jrank.org/pages/7165/Glass-Steagall-Act.html

[4] 82 Stat. 146.

[5] http://www.fdic.gov/regulations/laws/rules/6500-200.html

[6] 70 Stat. 133.

[7] Public Law 97-320.

[8] 105 Stat. 2236.

[9] 109 Stat. 271.

[10] Public Law 106-102, 113 Stat. 1338.

[11] David Corn, "Foreclosure Phil" July/August 2008, www.motherjones.com

[12] http://www.washingtonpost.com/wp-dyn/content/article/2008/10/20/AR
2008102003110_2.html?hpid=topnews&sub=new&sid=ST2008102100283&s_p

[13] www.responsiblelending.org/policy/congress/page.jsp?itemID=28009832

Bush Law: Emergency Economic Stabilization Act of 2008[1] (October 3, 2008)

Who is hurt by this law: People whose mortgages have been foreclosed, whose federal health and human services have ended, and millions who have lost their jobs. As of September 2008, 9.5 million are unemployed, officially 6.1%, not counting long-term unemployed.[2] A 2005 HUD study found 744,000 are homeless, of whom 41% are families.[3] Between 2008 and 2025, 78 million baby boomers will expect to live on Social Security. Taxpayers will lose the most, paying this debt for the next 20 years.

In 2000, "the U.S. had $5.7 trillion in total debt... only eight years later, that sum has nearly doubled, thanks to war costs, tax cuts, spending increases, expanded entitlement programs, and now a welter of government bailouts...."[4] "On March 16, 2007, Bear Stearns announced the takeover by JPMorgan Chase in Fed-engineered bailout... approved by Fed Bd. of Governors under a post-9/11 'national security emergency' exception."[5]

In April 2008, Business correspondent Bob Moon stated on American Public Media's Marketplace, "The value of the entire US Treasuries market: $4.5 trillion. The value of the entire mortgage market: $7 trillion. The size of the US stock market: $22 trillion. OK, you ready? The size of the credit default swap market last year:

155

$45 trillion... three times the whole US gross domestic product..."[6]
"The unregulated and poorly reported **credit default swaps ... were about $5 trillion more than the GDP of the entire world.**"[7]

What the Bush law provides: "... inject[s] capital directly into the major banks in exchange for equity. $125 billion is going into the first nine -- Goldman Sachs, Morgan Stanley, Merrill Lynch, Bank of America, Citigroup, JPMorgan Chase, Wells Fargo, and Bank of New York Mellon and State Street Corporation. This plus a guarantee of new debt over the next three years is designed to reassure other banks of their solvency, and hopefully get them to resume lending..."[8] Financial institutions have been lobbying to get a slice of the $700,000,000,000 federal bailout that has yet to help struggling homeowners.[9]

Current	Debt Held by the Public	Intragovernmental Holdings	Total Public Debt Outstanding
10/30/2008[10]	6,257,578,457,250	4,273,314,576,527	10,530,893,033,778

What the law provides: On October 3, 2008, Bush signed the modified bailout law introduced by Rep. Kennedy March 9, 2007. For more complete information, see note 1 and mcli.org.

- Increases the statutory limit on the public debt to $11.315 trillion and gives the Secretary of Treasury unprecedented power:

Troubled Assets Relief Program (TARP)

Authorizes Secretary of Treasury to purchase troubled assets from any financial institution, on terms he develops, including mortgage-backed securities issued before March 14, 2008.

What the "law" ignores:
- Glass-Steagall Act and other laws from the Depression Era
- U.S. Consitution general welfare clause; U.N. Charter Art. 55.

What Congress can do: In 2009, Congress can pass:
S. 2636: Foreclosure Prevention Act: (1) authorizes use of proceeds of qualified mortgage bond issue to refinance some

mortgages; (2) raises ceiling and volume cap imposed on certain state housing bonds; (3) excludes from meaning of tax preference item private activity bonds, for veterans' mortgage bonds issued after enactment of this Act and before January 1, 2011, etc. [11]

H.R. 5720: Housing Assistance Tax Act: Amends Internal Revenue Code re low-income housing tax credit and tax-exempt bond rules for financing low-income housing projects.[12]

---

[1] Public Law 110-343. To see the full text: http://frwebgate.access.gpo.gov/cgi-bin/getdoc.cgi?dbname=110_cong_bills&docid=f:h1424enr.txt.pdf

[2] U.S. Department of Labor, http://www.bls.gov/news.release/empsit.nr0.htm

[3] The Boston Globe; www.boston.com/news/nation/washington/articles/2007/01/11/of_744000_homeless_estimated_in_us_41_percent_are_in_families/

[4] David M. Walker, Former U.S. Comptroller General, "Call this a crisis? Just Wait," October 30, 2008, http://www.money.cnn.com/2008/10/28/magazines/fortune/babyboomcrisis_walker.fortune/index.htm

[5] Nomi Prins, "Where Credit is Due: a Timeline of the Mortgage Crisis," July/August 2008, http://www.motherjones.com/news/feature/2008/07/where-credit-is-due-timeline.html

[6] marketplace.publicradio.org/display/web/2008/04/01/credit_default_swaps_q

[7] Mark Sumner, "John McCain: Crisis Enabler,"September 21, 2008, The Nation, http://www.thenation.com/doc/20081006/sumner

[8] http://www.huffingtonpost.com/robert-l-borosage/in-paulson-we-trust_b_136591.html

[9] See "Bailout Bucks to Banks" list from Pro Publica, http://www.propublica.org/feature/bailout-bucks-to-banks-1028

[10] http://www.treasurydirect.gov/NP/BPDLogin?application=np

[11] To see the full text: http://www.govtrack.us/congress/bill.xpd?bill=s110-2636

[12] To see the full text: http://www.govtrack.us/congress/bill.xpd?bill=h110-5720

LAST MINUTE BUSH REGULATIONS INTO CODE OF FEDERAL REGULATIONS

Bush "Laws": "Midnight Regulations" issued by outgoing President on many controversial issues

What the Bush "laws" provide: In his final days in office, Bush issued a score of regulations on many very controversial issues that the new Obama Administration cannot quickly and easily repeal because they have been placed in the Code of Federal Regulations.[1]

- Permitting coal companies to drop waste from strip-mining into valleys
- Permitting coal-fired power stations to be built near national parks
- Allowing people to carry loaded and concealed weapons in national parks
- Opening up millions of acres to mining for oil shale
- Allowing health care workers to opt out of giving treatment (abortions, aid to AIDs victims) for religious or moral reasons
- Allowing truck drivers to stay at the wheel for 11 consecutive hours

What the "law" ignores: Major objections to each of these new regulations based on the U.S. Constitution general welfare clause, based on the existing wage and hour laws, on ecological studies, and based on the U.N. Charter Articles 55 and 56 human rights clauses.

What Congress can do: The House and Senate and federal Departments can start working to rescind each of these new regulations, but many require studies and hearings before they can be rescinded.

---

[1] From The Guradian-UK Dec. 14, 2008 by Paul Harris:
www.CommonDreams.org

158

APPENDIX

TEXT OF ALL PROVISIONS OF U.S. CONSTITUTION AND TREATIES CITED

United States Constitution
www.law.cornell.edu/constitution/constitution.table.html

Amendments to the Constitution
www.usconstitution.net/index.html

War Crimes Act
www4.law.cornell.edu/uscode/18/2441.html

Anti-Torture Statute
www.law.cornell.edu/uscode/18/usc_sup_01_18_10_I_20_113C.html

United Nations Charter
www.un.org/aboutun/charter/

Geneva Conventions Relative to the Treatment of Prisoners (of War)
www.unhchr.ch/html/menu3/b/91.htm

International Covenant on Civil and Political Rights (ICCPR)
www1.umn.edu/humanrts/instree/b3ccpr.htm

International Convention Against Torture and Other Cruel, Inhuman, or Degrading Treatment or Punishment (ICAT)
www.unhchr.ch/html/menu3/b/h_cat39.htm

International Convention on the Elimination of all Forms of Racial Discrimination (ICERD)
www2.ohchr.org/html/english/law/cerd.htm

Optional Protocol to the Convention on the Rights of the Child on the Involvement of Children in Armed Conflict
www.unhchr.ch/html/menu2/6/protocolchild.htm

Convention on the Rights of the Child
www.unhchr.ch/html/menu3/b/k2crc.htm

United States Constitution

Preamble: We the People of the United States, in Order to form a more perfect Union, establish Justice, insure domestic Tranquility, provide for the common defence, promote the general Welfare,

159

and secure the Blessings of Liberty to ourselves and our Posterity, do ordain and establish this Constitution for the United States of America.

Article 1, Section 2, Cl 1: The House of Representatives shall be composed of Members chosen every second Year by the People of the several States, and the Electors in each State shall have the Qualifications requisite for Electors of the most numerous Branch of the State Legislature.

Article 1, Section 2, Cl 2: No Person shall be a Representative who shall not have attained to the Age of twenty five Years, and been seven Years a Citizen of the United States, and who shall not, when elected, be an Inhabitant of that State in which he shall be chosen.

Article 1, Section 2, Cl 3: Representatives and direct Taxes shall be apportioned among the several States which may be included within this Union, according to their respective Numbers, which shall be determined by adding to the whole Number of free Persons, including those bound to Service for a Term of Years, and excluding Indians not taxed, three fifths of all other Persons. The actual Enumeration shall be made within three Years after the first Meeting of the Congress of the United States, and within every subsequent Term of ten Years, in such Manner as they shall by Law direct. The Number of Representatives shall not exceed one for every thirty Thousand, but each State shall have at Least one Representative; and until such enumeration shall be made, the State of New Hampshire shall be entitled to chuse three, Massachusetts eight, Rhode-Island and Providence Plantations one, Connecticut five, New-York six, New Jersey four, Pennsylvania eight, Delaware one, Maryland six, Virginia ten, North Carolina five, South Carolina five, and Georgia three.

Article 1, Section 2, Cl 4: When vacancies happen in the Representation from any State, the Executive Authority thereof shall issue Writs of Election to fill such Vacancies.

Article 1, Section 2, Cl 5: The House of Representatives shall choose their Speaker and other Officers; and shall have the sole Power of Impeachment.

Article 1, Section 8, Cl 1: (General Welfare Clause) The Congress shall have Power To lay and collect Taxes, Duties, Imposts and

Excises, to pay the Debts and provide for the common Defence and general Welfare of the United States; but all Duties, Imposts and Excises shall be uniform throughout the United States; ...

Article 1, Section 8, Cl 11: To declare War, grant Letters of Marque and Reprisal, and make Rules concerning Captures on Land and Water;

Article 1, Section 8, Cl 12: To raise and support Armies, but no Appropriation of Money to that Use shall be for a longer Term than two Years;...

Article 1, Section 9, Cl 1: The Migration or Importation of such Persons as any of the States now existing shall think proper to admit, shall not be prohibited by the Congress prior to the Year one thousand eight hundred and eight, but a Tax or duty may be imposed on such Importation, not exceeding ten dollars for each Person.

Article 1, Section 9, Cl 2: The Privilege of the Writ of Habeas Corpus shall not be suspended, unless when in Cases of Rebellion or Invasion the public Safety may require it.

Article 1, Section 9, Cl 7: No Money shall be drawn from the Treasury, but in Consequence of Appropriations made by Law; and a regular Statement and Account of the Receipts and Expenditures of all public Money shall be published from time to time.

Article 2, Section 1, Cl 8: Before he enter on the Execution of his Office, he shall take the following Oath or Affirmation:--"I do solemnly swear (or affirm) that I will faithfully execute the Office of President of the United States, and will to the best of my Ability, preserve, protect and defend the Constitution of the United States."

Article 2, Section 3: He shall from time to time give to the Congress Information of the State of the Union, and recommend to their Consideration such Measures as he shall judge necessary and expedient; he may, on extraordinary Occasions, convene both Houses, or either of them, and in Case of Disagreement between them, with Respect to the Time of Adjournment, he may adjourn them to such Time as he shall think proper; he shall receive Ambassadors and other public Ministers; he shall take Care that the Laws be faithfully executed, and shall Commission all the Officers of the United States.

161

Article 6, Section 2: This Constitution, and the Laws of the United States which shall be made in Pursuance thereof; and all Treaties made, or which shall be made, under the Authority of the United States, shall be the supreme Law of the Land; and the Judges in every State shall be bound thereby, anything in the Constitution or Laws of any State to the Contrary notwithstanding.

Amendments to the Constitution

Article I: Congress shall make no law respecting an establishment of religion, or prohibiting the free exercise thereof; or abridging the freedom of speech, or of the press; or the right of the people peaceably to assemble, and to petition the Government for a redress of grievances.

Article IV: The right of the people to be secure in their persons, houses, papers, and effects, against unreasonable searches and seizures, shall not be violated, and no Warrants shall issue, but upon probable cause, supported by Oath or affirmation, and particularly describing the place to be searched, and the persons or things to be seized.

Article V: No person shall be held to answer for a capital, or otherwise infamous crime, unless on a presentment or indictment of a Grand Jury, except in cases arising in the land or naval forces, or in the Militia, when in actual service in time of War or public danger; nor shall any person be subject for the same offence to be twice put in jeopardy of life or limb; nor shall be compelled in any criminal case to be a witness against himself, nor be deprived of life, liberty, or property, without due process of law; nor shall private property be taken for public use, without just compensation.

Article VI: In all criminal prosecutions, the accused shall enjoy the right to a speedy and public trial, by an impartial jury of the State and district wherein the crime shall have been committed, which district shall have been previously ascertained by law, and to be informed of the nature and cause of the accusation; to be confronted with the witnesses against him; to have compulsory process for obtaining witnesses in his favor, and to have the Assistance of Counsel for his defence.

Article VIII: Excessive bail shall not be required, nor excessive fines imposed, nor cruel and unusual punishments inflicted.

Article IX: The enumeration in the Constitution, of certain rights, shall not be construed to deny or disparage others retained by the people.

Article X: The powers not delegated to the United States by the Constitution, nor prohibited by it to the States, are reserved to the States respectively, or to the people.

Article XIV, 1: All persons born or naturalized in the United States, and subject to the jurisdiction thereof, are citizens of the United States and of the State wherein they reside. No State shall make or enforce any law which shall abridge the privileges or immunities of citizens of the United States; nor shall any State deprive any person of life, liberty, or property, without due process of law; nor deny to any person within its jurisdiction the equal protection of the laws.

Article XIV, 2: Representatives shall be apportioned among the several States according to their respective numbers, counting the whole number of persons in each State, excluding Indians not taxed. But when the right to vote at any election for the choice of electors for President and Vice President of the United States, Representatives in Congress, the Executive and Judicial officers of a State, or the members of the Legislature thereof, is denied to any of the male inhabitants of such State, being twenty-one years of age, and citizens of the United States, or in any way abridged, except for participation in rebellion, or other crime, the basis of representation therein shall be reduced in the proportion which the number of such male citizens shall bear to the whole number of male citizens twenty-one years of age in such State.

Article XIV, 3: No person shall be a Senator or Representative in Congress, or elector of President and Vice President, or hold any office, civil or military, under the United States, or under any State, who, having previously taken an oath, as a member of Congress, or as an officer of the United States, or as a member of any State legislature, or as an executive or judicial officer of any State, to support the Constitution of the United States, shall have engaged in insurrection or rebellion against the same, or given aid or comfort to the enemies thereof. But Congress may by a vote of two-thirds of each House, remove such disability.

Article XIV, 4: The validity of the public debt of the United States, authorized by law, including debts incurred for payment of pensions and bounties for services in suppressing insurrection or

163

rebellion, shall not be questioned. But neither the United States nor any State shall assume or pay any debt or obligation incurred in aid of insurrection or rebellion against the United States, or any claim for the loss or emancipation of any slave; but all such debts, obligations and claims shall be held illegal and void.

Article XIV, 5: The Congress shall have power to enforce, by appropriate legislation, the provisions of this article.

War Crimes Act

U. S. Code, Title 18, Part 1, Chapter 118, Section 2441, Subsections A and B: (A)Offense -- Whoever, whether inside or outside the United States, commits a war crime, in any of the circumstances described in subsection (b), shall be fined under this title or imprisoned for life or any term of years, or both, and if death results to the victim, shall also be subject to the penalty of death. (B) Circumstances. -- The circumstances referred to in subsection (a) are that the person committing such war crime or the victim of such war crime is a member of the Armed Forces of the United States or a national of the United States (as defined in section 101 of the Immigration and Nationality Act). (c) Definition. — As used in this section the term "war crime" means any conduct—
(1) defined as a grave breach in any of the international lconventions signed at Geneva 12 August 1949, or any protocol to such convention to which the United States is a party;_

Anti-Torture Statute

U. S. Code, Title 18, Part 1, Chapter 113c, Section 2340, Subsection A: Offense.--Whoever outside the United States commits or attempts to commit torture shall be fined under this title or imprisoned not more than 20 years, or both, and if death results to any person from conduct prohibited by this subsection, shall be punished by death or imprisoned for any term of years or for life.

(1)"torture" means an act committed by a person acting under the color of law specifically intended to inflict severe physical or mental pain or suffering (other than pain or suffering incidental to lawful sanctions) upon another person within his custody or physical control.

United Nations Charter

Preamble: We the peoples of the United Nations Determined to save succeeding generations from the scourge of war, which twice in our lifetime has brought untold sorrow to mankind, and to reaffirm faith in fundamental human rights, in the dignity and worth of the human person, in the equal rights of men and women and of nations large and small, and to establish conditions under which justice and respect for the obligations arising from treaties and other sources of international law can be maintained, and to promote social progress and better standards of life in larger freedom and for these ends to practice tolerance and live together in peace with one another as good neighbours, and to unite our strength to maintain international peace and security, and to ensure, by the acceptance of principles and the institution of methods, that armed force shall not be used, save in the common interest, and to employ international machinery for the promotion of the economic and social advancement of all peoples, have resolved to combine our efforts to accomplish these aims.

Accordingly, our respective Governments, through representatives assembled in the city of San Francisco, who have exhibited their full powers found to be in good and due form, have agreed to the present Charter of the United Nations and do hereby establish an international organization to be known as the United Nations.

Article 1: The Purposes of the United Nations are **(1)** To maintain international peace and security, and to that end: to take effective collective measures for the prevention and removal of threats to the peace, and for the suppression of acts of aggression or other breaches of the peace, and to bring about by peaceful means, and in conformity with the principles of justice and international law, adjustment or settlement of international disputes or situations which might lead to a breach of the peace; **(2)** To develop friendly relations among nations based on respect for the principle of equal rights and self-determination of peoples, and to take other appropriate measures to strengthen universal peace; **(3)** To achieve international co-operation in solving international problems of an economic, social, cultural, or humanitarian character, and in promoting and encouraging respect for human rights and for fundamental freedoms for all without distinction as to race, sex, language, or religion; and **(4)** To be a centre for harmonizing the actions of nations in the attainment of these common ends.

Article 2: The Organization and its Members, in pursuit of the Purposes stated in Article 1, shall act in accordance with the following Principles.**(1)** The Organization is based on the principle of the sovereign equality of all its Members. **(2)** All Members, in order to ensure to all of them the rights and benefits resulting from membership, shall fulfill in good faith the obligations assumed by them in accordance with the present Charter. **(3)** All Members shall settle their international disputes by peaceful means in such a manner that international peace and security, and justice, are not endangered. **(4)** All Members shall refrain in their international relations from the threat or use of force against the territorial integrity or political independence of any state, or in any other manner inconsistent with the Purposes of the United Nations. **(5)** All Members shall give the United Nations every assistance in any action it takes in accordance with the present Charter, and shall refrain from giving assistance to any state against which the United Nations is taking preventive or enforcement action. **(6)** The Organization shall ensure that states which are not Members of the United Nations act in accordance with these Principles so far as may be necessary for the maintenance of international peace and security. **(7)** Nothing contained in the present Charter shall authorize the United Nations to intervene in matters which are essentially within the domestic jurisdiction of any state or shall require the Members to submit such matters to settlement under the present Charter; but this principle shall not prejudice the application of enforcement measures under Chapter VII.

Article 33, 1: The parties to any dispute, the continuance of which is likely to endanger the maintenance of international peace and security, shall, first of all, seek a solution by negotiation, enquiry, mediation, conciliation, arbitration, judicial settlement, resort to regional agencies or arrangements, or other peaceful means of their own choice.

Article 37, 1: Should the parties to a dispute of the nature referred to in Article 33 fail to settle it by the means indicated in that Article, they shall refer it to the Security Council.

Article 39: The Security Council shall determine the existence of any threat to the peace, breach of the peace, or act of aggression and shall make recommendations, or decide what measures shall be taken in accordance with Articles 41 and 42, to maintain or restore international peace and security.

Article 55: With a view to the creation of conditions of stability and well-being which are necessary for peaceful and friendly relations among nations based on respect for the principle of equal rights and self-determination of peoples, the United Nations shall promote:

(a) higher standards of living, full employment, and conditions of economic and social progress and development;

(b) solutions of international economic, social, health, and related problems; and international cultural and educational cooperation; and

(c) universal respect for, and observance of, human rights and fundamental freedoms for all without distinction as to race, sex, language, or religion.

Article 56: All Members pledge themselves to take joint and separate action in co-operation with the Organization for the achievement of the purposes set forth in Article 55

Geneva Conventions Relative to the Treatment of Prisoners (of War)

Article 118: Prisoners of war shall be released and repatriated without delay after the cessation of active hostilities. In the absence of stipulations to the above effect in any agreement concluded between the Parties to the conflict with a view to the cessation of hostilities, or failing any such agreement, each of the Detaining Powers shall itself establish and execute without delay a plan of repatriation in conformity with the principle laid down in the foregoing paragraph. In either case, the measures adopted shall be brought to the knowledge of the prisoners of war. The costs of repatriation of prisoners of war shall in all cases be equitably apportioned between the Detaining Power and the Power on which the prisoners depend. This apportionment shall be carried out on the following basis: (a) If the two Powers are contiguous, the Power on which the prisoners of war depend shall bear the costs of repatriation from the frontiers of the Detaining Power. (b) If the two Powers are not contiguous, the Detaining Power shall bear the costs of transport of prisoners of war over its own territory as far as its frontier or its port of embarkation nearest to the territory of the Power on which the prisoners of war depend. The Parties concerned shall agree between themselves as to the equitable apportionment of the remaining costs of the repatriation. The conclusion of this agreement shall in no circumstances justify any delay in the repatriation of the prisoners of war.

International Covenant on Civil and Political Rights (ICCPR)

Preamble: The States Parties to the present Covenant, Considering that, in accordance with the principles proclaimed in the Charter of the United Nations, recognition of the inherent dignity and of the equal and inalienable rights of all members of the human family is the foundation of freedom, justice and peace in the world,

Recognizing that these rights derive from the inherent dignity of the human person,

Recognizing that, in accordance with the Universal Declaration of Human Rights, the ideal of free human beings enjoying civil and political freedom and freedom from fear and want can only be achieved if conditions are created whereby everyone may enjoy his civil and political rights, as well as his economic, social and cultural rights,

Considering the obligation of States under the Charter of the United Nations to promote universal respect for, and observance of, human rights and freedoms,

Realizing that the individual, having duties to other individuals and to the community to which he belongs, is under a responsibility to strive for the promotion and observance of the rights recognized in the present Covenant, Agree upon the following articles:

Article 1, 1: All peoples have the right of self-determination. By virtue of that right they freely determine their political status and freely pursue their economic, social and cultural development.

Article 1, 2: All peoples may, for their own ends, freely dispose of their natural wealth and resources without prejudice to any obligations arising out of international economic co-operation, based upon the principle of mutual benefit, and international law. In no case may a people be deprived of its own means of subsistence.

168

Article 2, 1: Each State Party to the present Covenant undertakes to respect and to ensure to all individuals within its territory and subject to its jurisdiction the rights recognized in the present Covenant, without distinction of any kind, such as race, colour, sex, language, religion, political or other opinion, national or social origin, property, birth or other status.

Article 6, 1: Every human being has the inherent right to life. This right shall be protected by law. No one shall be arbitrarily deprived of his life.

Article 6, 2: In countries which have not abolished the death penalty, sentence of death may be imposed only for the most serious crimes in accordance with the law in force at the time of the commission of the crime and not contrary to the provisions of the present Covenant and to the Convention on the Prevention and Punishment of the Crime of Genocide. This penalty can only be carried out pursuant to a final judgement rendered by a competent court.

Article 6, 3: When deprivation of life constitutes the crime of genocide, it is understood that nothing in this article shall authorize any State Party to the present Covenant to derogate in any way from any obligation assumed under the provisions of the Convention on the Prevention and Punishment of the Crime of Genocide.

Article 6, 4: Anyone sentenced to death shall have the right to seek pardon or commutation of the sentence. Amnesty, pardon or commutation of the sentence of death may be granted in all cases.

Article 6, 5: Sentence of death shall not be imposed for crimes committed by persons below eighteen years of age and shall not be carried out on pregnant women.

Article 6, 6: Nothing in this article shall be invoked to delay or to prevent the abolition of capital punishment by any State Party to the present Covenant.

Article 7: No one shall be subjected to torture or to cruel, inhuman or degrading treatment or punishment. In particular, no one shall be subjected without his free consent to medical or scientific experimentation.

Article 9, 1: Everyone has the right to liberty and security of person. No one shall be subjected to arbitrary arrest or detention. No one shall be deprived of his liberty except on such grounds and in accordance with such procedure as are established by law.

Article 9, 2: Anyone who is arrested shall be informed, at the time of arrest, of the reasons for his arrest and shall be promptly informed of any charges against him.

Article 10, 1: All persons deprived of their liberty shall be treated with humanity and with respect for the inherent dignity of the human person.

Article 10, 2, (a): Accused person shall, save in exceptional circumstances, be segregated from convicted persons and shall be subject to separate treatment appropriate to their status as unconvicted persons;

Article 10, 2, (b): Accused juvenile persons shall be separated from adults and brought as speedily as possible for adjudication.

Article 10, 3: The penitentiary system shall comprise treatment of prisoners the essential aim of which shall be their reformation and social rehabilitation. Juvenile offenders shall be segregated from adults and be accorded treatment appropriate to their age and legal status.

Article 12, 1: Everyone lawfully within the territory of a State shall, within that territory, have the right to liberty of movement and freedom to choose his residence.

Article 14, 3: In the determination of any criminal charge against him, everyone shall be entitled to the following minimum guarantees, in full equality: (a) To be informed promptly and in detail in a language which he understands of the nature and cause of the charge against him; (b) To have adequate time and facilities for the preparation of his defence and to communicate with counsel of his own choosing; (c) To be tried without undue delay; (d) To be tried in his presence, and to defend himself in person or through legal assistance of his own choosing; to be informed, if he does not have legal assistance, of this right; and to have legal assistance assigned to him, in any case where the interests of justice so require, and without payment by him in any such case if he does not have sufficient means to pay for it; (e) To examine, or have examined, the witnesses against him and to obtain the attendance and examination of witnesses on his behalf under the same conditions as witnesses against him; (f) To have the free assistance of an interpreter if he cannot understand or speak the language used in court; (g) Not to be compelled to testify against himself or to confess guilt.

170

Article 14, 4: In the case of juvenile persons, the procedure shall be such as will take account of their age and the desirability of promoting their rehabilitation.

Article 14, 5: Everyone convicted of a crime shall have the right to his conviction and sentence being reviewed by a higher tribunal according to law.

Article 14, 6: When a person has by a final decision been convicted of a criminal offence and when subsequently his conviction has been reversed or he has been pardoned on the ground that a new or newly discovered fact shows conclusively that there has been a miscarriage of justice, the person who has suffered punishment as a result of such conviction shall be compensated according to law, unless it is proved that the non-disclosure of the unknown fact in time is wholly or partly attributable to him.

Article 14, 7: No one shall be liable to be tried or punished again for an offence for which he has already been finally convicted or acquitted in accordance with the law and penal procedure of each country.

Article 16: Everyone shall have the right to recognition everywhere as a person before the law.

Article 17, 1: No one shall be subjected to arbitrary or unlawful interference with his privacy, family, or correspondence, nor to unlawful attacks on his honour and reputation.

Article 18, 1: Everyone shall have the right to freedom of thought, conscience and religion. This right shall include freedom to have or to adopt a religion or belief of his choice, and freedom, either individually or in community with others and in public or private, to manifest his religion or belief in worship, observance, practice and teaching.

Article 19, 1: Everyone shall have the right to hold opinions without interference.

Article 19, 2: Everyone shall have the right to freedom of expression; this right shall include freedom to seek, receive and impart information and ideas of all kinds, regardless of frontiers, either orally, in writing or in print, in the form of art, or through any other media of his choice.

Article 22, 1: Everyone shall have the right to freedom of association with others, including the right to form and join trade unions for the protection of his interests.

Article 23, 1: The family is the natural and fundamental group unit of society and is entitled to protection by society and the State.

Article 24, 1: Every child shall have, without any discrimination as to race, colour, sex, language, religion, national or social origin, property or birth, the right to such measures of protection as are required by his status as a minor, on the part of his family, society and the State.

Article 24, 2: Every child shall be registered immediately after birth and shall have a name.

Article 25: Every citizen shall have the right and the opportunity, without any of the distinctions mentioned in article 2 and without unreasonable restrictions: (a) To take part in the conduct of public affairs, directly or through freely chosen representatives; (b) To vote and to be elected at genuine periodic elections which shall be by universal and equal suffrage and shall be held by secret ballot, guaranteeing the free expression of the will of the electors;...

Article 26: All persons are equal before the law and are entitled without any discrimination to the equal protection of the law. In this respect, the law shall prohibit any discrimination and guarantee to all persons equal and effective protection against discrimination on any ground such as race, colour, sex, language, religion, political or other opinion, national or social origin, property, birth or other status.

International Convention Against Torture and Other Cruel, Inhuman, or Degrading Treatment or Punishment (ICAT)

Article 2, 1: Each State Party shall take effective legislative, administrative, judicial or other measures to prevent acts of torture in any territory under its jurisdiction.

Article 2, 2: No exceptional circumstances whatsoever, whether a state of war or a threat of war, internal political in stability or any other public emergency, may be invoked as a justification of torture.

Article 2, 3: An order from a superior officer or a public authority may not be invoked as a justification of torture.

172

Article 3, 1: No State Party shall expel, return ("refouler") or extradite a person to another State where there are substantial grounds for believing that he would be in danger of being subjected to torture.

Article 3, 2: For the purpose of determining whether there are such grounds, the competent authorities shall take into account all relevant considerations including, where applicable, the existence in the State concerned of a consistent pattern of gross, flagrant or mass violations of human rights.

Article 5, 1: Each State Party shall take such measures as may be necessary to establish its jurisdiction over the offences referred to in article 4 in the following cases: (a) When the offences are committed in any territory under its jurisdiction or on board a ship or aircraft registered in that State; (b) When the alleged offender is a national of that State;...

Article 6, 1: Upon being satisfied, after an examination of information available to it, that the circumstances so warrant, any State Party in whose territory a person alleged to have committed any offence referred to in article 4 is present shall take him into custody or take other legal measures to ensure his presence. The custody and other legal measures shall be as provided in the law of that State but may be continued only for such time as is necessary to enable any criminal or extradition proceedings to be instituted.

Article 6, 2: Such State shall immediately make a preliminary inquiry into the facts.

Article 6, 3: Any person in custody pursuant to paragraph I of this article shall be assisted in communicating immediately with the nearest appropriate representative of the State of which he is a national, or, if he is a stateless person, with the representative of the State where he usually resides.

Article 6, 4: When a State, pursuant to this article, has taken a person into custody, it shall immediately notify the States referred to in article 5, paragraph 1, of the fact that such person is in custody and of the circumstances which warrant his detention. The State which makes the preliminary inquiry contemplated in paragraph 2 of this article shall promptly report its findings to the said States and shall indicate whether it intends to exercise jurisdiction.

Article 7, 1: The State Party in the territory under whose jurisdiction a person alleged to have committed any offence referred to in article 4 is found shall in the cases contemplated in article 5, if it does not extradite him, submit the case to its competent authorities for the purpose of prosecution.

Article 7, 2: These authorities shall take their decision in the same manner as in the case of any ordinary offence of a serious nature under the law of that State. In the cases referred to in article 5, paragraph 2, the standards of evidence required for prosecution and conviction shall in no way be less stringent than those which apply in the cases referred to in article 5, paragraph 1.

Article 7, 3: Any person regarding whom proceedings are brought in connection with any of the offences referred to in article 4 shall be guaranteed fair treatment at all stages of the proceedings.

Article 10, 1: Each State Party shall ensure that education and information regarding the prohibition against torture are fully included in the training of law enforcement personnel, civil or military, medical personnel, public officials and other persons who may be involved in the custody, interrogation or treatment of any individual subjected to any form of arrest, detention or imprisonment.

Article 11: Each State Party shall keep under systematic review interrogation rules, instructions, methods and practices as well as arrangements for the custody and treatment of persons subjected to any form of arrest, detention or imprisonment in any territory under its jurisdiction, with a view to preventing any cases of torture.

Article 16, 1: Each State Party shall undertake to prevent in any territory under its jurisdiction other acts of cruel, inhuman or degrading treatment or punishment which do not amount to torture as defined in article I, when such acts are committed by or at the instigation of or with the consent or acquiescence of a public official or other person acting in an official capacity. In particular, the obligations contained in articles 10, 11, 12 and 13 shall apply with the substitution for references to torture of references to other forms of cruel, inhuman or degrading treatment or punishment.

International Convention on the Elimination of all Forms of Racial Discrimination (ICERD)

Preamble: The States Parties to this Convention, Considering that the Charter of the United Nations is based on the principles of the dignity and equality inherent in all human beings, and that all Member States have pledged themselves to take joint and separate action, in co-operation with the Organization, for the achievement of one of the purposes of the United Nations which is to promote and encourage universal respect for and observance of human rights and fundamental freedoms for all, without distinction as to race, sex, language or religion,

Considering that the Universal Declaration of Human Rights proclaims that all human beings are born free and equal in dignity and rights and that everyone is entitled to all the rights and freedoms set out therein, without distinction of any kind, in particular as to race, colour or national origin,

Considering that all human beings are equal before the law and are entitled to equal protection of the law against any discrimination and against any incitement to discrimination,

Considering that the United Nations has condemned colonialism and all practices of segregation and discrimination associated therewith, in whatever form and wherever they exist, and that the Declaration on the Granting of Independence to Colonial Countries and Peoples of 14 December 1960 (General Assembly resolution 1514 (XV)) has affirmed and solemnly proclaimed the necessity of bringing them to a speedy and unconditional end,

Considering that the United Nations Declaration on the Elimination of All Forms of Racial Discrimination of 20 November 1963 (General Assembly resolution 1904 (XVIII)) solemnly affirms the necessity of speedily eliminating racial discrimination throughout the world in all its forms and manifestations and of securing understanding of and respect for the dignity of the human person,

Convinced that any doctrine of superiority based on racial differentiation is scientifically false, morally condemnable, socially unjust and dangerous, and that there is no justification for racial discrimination, in theory or in practice, anywhere,

175

Reaffirming that discrimination between human beings on the grounds of race, colour or ethnic origin is an obstacle to friendly and peaceful relations among nations and is capable of disturbing peace and security among peoples and the harmony of persons living side by side even within one and the same State,

Convinced that the existence of racial barriers is repugnant to the ideals of any human society, Alarmed by manifestations of racial discrimination still in evidence in some areas of the world and by governmental policies based on racial superiority or hatred, such as policies of apartheid, segregation or separation,

Resolved to adopt all necessary measures for speedily eliminating racial discrimination in all its forms and manifestations, and to prevent and combat racist doctrines and practices in order to promote understanding between races and to build an international community free from all forms of racial segregation and racial discrimination,

Bearing in mind the Convention concerning Discrimination in respect of Employment and Occupation adopted by the International Labour Organisation in 1958, and the Convention against Discrimination in Education adopted by the United Nations Educational, Scientific and Cultural Organization in 1960,

Desiring to implement the principles embodied in the United Nations Declaration on the Elimination of All Forms of Racial Discrimination and to secure the earliest adoption of practical measures to that end,

Have agreed as follows:

Part 1, Article 1, Section 1: In this Convention, the term "racial discrimination" shall mean any distinction, exclusion, restriction or preference based on race, colour, descent, or national or ethnic origin which has the purpose or effect of nullifying or impairing the recognition, enjoyment or exercise, on an equal footing, of human rights and fundamental freedoms in the political, economic, social, cultural or any other field of public life.

Article 2, 1: States Parties condemn racial discrimination and undertake to pursue by all appropriate means and without delay a policy of eliminating racial discrimination in all its forms and promoting understanding among all races, and, to this end: (a) Each State Party undertakes to engage in no act or practice

176

of racial discrimination against persons, groups of persons or institutions and to ensure that all public authorities and public institutions, national and local, shall act in conformity with this obligation; (b) Each State Party undertakes not to sponsor, defend or support racial discrimination by any persons or organizations; (c) Each State Party shall take effective measures to review governmental, national and local policies, and to amend, rescind or nullify any laws and regulations which have the effect of creating or perpetuating racial discrimination wherever it exists; (d) Each State Party shall prohibit and bring to an end, by all appropriate means, including legislation as required by circumstances, racial discrimination by any persons, group or organization; (e) Each State Party undertakes to encourage, where appropriate, integrationist multiracial organizations and movements and other means of eliminating barriers between races, and to discourage anything which tends to strengthen racial division.

Article 2, 2: States Parties shall, when the circumstances so warrant, take, in the social, economic, cultural and other fields, special and concrete measures to ensure the adequate development and protection of certain racial groups or individuals belonging to them, for the purpose of guaranteeing them the full and equal enjoyment of human rights and fundamental freedoms. These measures shall in no case entail as a consequence the maintenance of unequal or separate rights for different racial groups after the objectives for which they were taken have been achieved.

Article 5: In compliance with the fundamental obligations laid down in article 2 of this Convention, States Parties undertake to prohibit and to eliminate racial discrimination in all its forms and to guarantee the right of everyone, without distinction as to race, colour, or national or ethnic origin, to equality before the law, notably in the enjoyment of the following rights: (a) The right to equal treatment before the tribunals and all other organs administering justice; (b) The right to security of person and protection by the State against violence or bodily harm, whether inflicted by government officials or by any individual group or institution; (c) Political rights, in particular the right to participate in elections-to vote and to stand for election-on the basis of universal and equal suffrage, to take part in the Government as well as in the conduct of public affairs at any level and to have equal access to public service; (d) Other civil rights, in particular: (i) The right to freedom of movement and residence within the border of the State; (ii) The right to leave any country, including one's own, and to return to one's country; (iii) The right to nationality; (iv) The right to marriage and choice of spouse; (v) The right to own property alone as well as in association with others; (vi) The right to inherit; (vii) The right to freedom of thought, conscience and religion; (viii) The right to freedom of opinion and expression; (ix) The right to freedom of peaceful assembly and association; (e) Economic, social and cultural rights, in particular: (i) The rights to work, to free choice of employment, to just and favourable conditions of work, to protection against unemployment, to equal pay for equal work, to just and favourable remuneration; (ii) The right to form and join trade unions; (iii) The right to housing; (iv) The right to public health, medical care, social security and social services; (v) The right to education and training; (vi) The right to equal participation in cultural activities; (f) The right of access to any place or service intended for use by the general public, such as transport hotels, restaurants, cafes, theatres and parks.

Article 16: The provisions of this Convention concerning the settlement of disputes or complaints shall be applied without prejudice to other procedures for settling disputes or complaints in the field of discrimination laid down in the constituent instruments of, or conventions adopted by, the United Nations and its specialized agencies, and shall not prevent the States Parties from having recourse to other procedures for settling a dispute in accordance with general or special international agreements in force between them.

Optional Protocol to the Convention on the Rights of the Child on the Involvement of Children in Armed Conflict

Article 3, 3: States Parties that permit voluntary recruitment into their national armed forces under the age of 18 years shall maintain safeguards to ensure, as a minimum, that: (a) Such recruitment is genuinely voluntary; (b) Such recruitment is carried out with the informed consent of the person's parents or legal guardians; (c) Such persons are fully informed of the duties involved in such military service; (d) Such persons provide reliable proof of age prior to acceptance into national military service.

Convention on the Rights of the Child
(Signed by the U.S. but not yet Ratified)

Article 2, 1: States Parties shall respect and ensure the rights set forth in the present Convention to each child within their jurisdiction without discrimination of any kind, irrespective of the child's or his or her parent's or legal guardian's race, colour, sex, language, religion, political or other opinion, national, ethnic or social origin, property, disability, birth or other status.

Article 3, 1: In all actions concerning children, whether undertaken by public or private social welfare institutions, courts of law, administrative authorities or legislative bodies, the best interests of the child shall be a primary consideration.

Article 5: States Parties shall respect the responsibilities, rights and duties of parents or, where applicable, the members of the extended family or community as provided for by local custom, legal guardians or other persons legally responsible for the child, to provide, in a manner consistent with the evolving capacities of the child, appropriate direction and guidance in the exercise by the child of the rights recognized in the present Convention.

Article 13, 1: The child shall have the right to freedom of expression; this right shall include freedom to seek, receive and impart information and ideas of all kinds, regardless of frontiers, either orally, in writing or in print, in the form of art, or through any other media of the child's choice.

Article 28, 1: States Parties recognize the right of the child to education, and with a view to achieving this right progressively and on the basis of equal opportunity, they shall, in particular: (a) Make primary education compulsory and available free to all; (b) Encourage the development of different forms of secondary education, including general and vocational education, make them available and accessible to every child, and take appropriate measures such as the introduction of free education and offering financial assistance in case of need; (c) Make higher education accessible to all on the basis of capacity by every appropriate means; (d) Make educational and vocational information and guidance available and accessible to all children; (e) Take measures to encourage regular attendance at schools and the reduction of drop-out rates.

INDEX TO STATUTES, BILLS, EXECUTIVE ORDERS AND SIGNING STATEMENTS

Note: In order to access the full text of the bills listed in the text, log onto www.gov.track.us. Type the bill number and year in the Bill Search box. It will provide a summary and full text of the bill, the status of the bill, and the voting records on each bill in the Senate and House of Representatives.

Bills introduced but not passed by Congress are often labeled Acts. Here they are all listed as Bills. The character *"f"* indicates that the reference continues beyond the page cited.

Signing Statements and Executive Orders and Model State Laws and Code of Federal Regulations changes are in italics.

INDEX OF SENATORS AND
REPRESENTATIVES WHO INTRODUCED
BILLS

To find the Washington, D.C. and Home Office addresses, phone numbers, email addresses, etc. of each Senator and Representative, visit http://www.congress.org